T0277950

TRAVELS THROUGH THE
HEART & SOUL
OF NEW ENGLAND

TRAVELS THROUGH THE
HEART ⁊ SOUL
OF NEW ENGLAND

Stories of Struggle, Resilience, and Triumph

Ted Reinstein

Globe
Pequot

Essex, Connecticut

Globe
Pequot

An imprint of Globe Pequot, the trade division of
The Rowman & Littlefield Publishing Group, Inc.
4501 Forbes Blvd., Ste. 200
Lanham, MD 20706
www.rowman.com

Distributed by NATIONAL BOOK NETWORK

Copyright © 2024 by Ted Reinstein
Photography by Ted Reinstein unless otherwise noted.

All rights reserved. No part of this book may be reproduced in any form or by any electronic or mechanical means, including information storage and retrieval systems, without written permission from the publisher, except by a reviewer who may quote passages in a review.

British Library Cataloguing in Publication Information available

Library of Congress Cataloging-in-Publication Data
9781493076093 (paper)
9781493076109 (electronic book text)

♾️™ The paper used in this publication meets the minimum requirements of American National Standard for Information Sciences—Permanence of Paper for Printed Library Materials, ANSI/NISO Z39.48-1992.

TABLE of CONTENTS

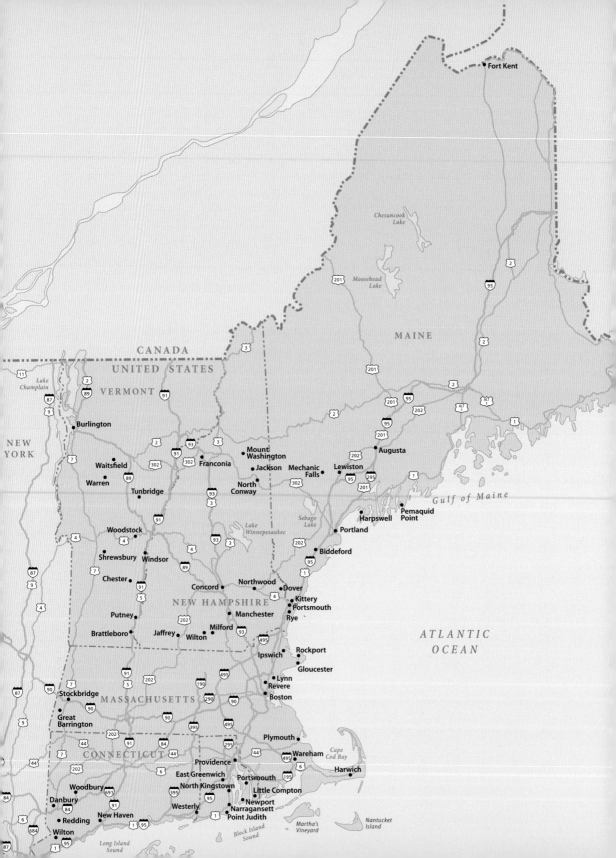

PREFACE

America's northeast corner is a special place. New England. In all its non-newness. All its non-Englishness. Although, among just three of its six states, you'll find Manchester, New London, Dover, Oxford, Cambridge, Canterbury, and Cornwall. Guess that counts as a wee bit English. (There's even a Liverpool, though it's in New York. Which means, for a New Englander, it doesn't count.)

But still.

Here, some of the first Europeans and white settlers disembarked and made their mark. Here the seeds of American independence were first sown, and here the battle to create a new nation began. Here such great American institutions as public parks, beaches, public schools, and public libraries all were born. (Not to mention diners.)

And here, the original natives of the land would come to rue the day they'd helped those first Europeans survive their first punishing winter.

But still.

It is America's oldest clearly defined region. It's small. Its six states together would fit into California more than twice. Its smallest state alone–Rhode Island–would fit into Texas 221 times.

Yet, for a small place, New England's had a big history. Over four hundred years of European settlement; as much as twelve thousand years of Indigenous presence. For a small place, it's exerted an outsized influence. Through the struggle for independence and well into America's development as an industrial nation, New England figured significantly and repeatedly in pivotal events, inventions, and social movements. Noteworthy New England men and women have been celebrated across all areas of American life, from industry and education to literature, science, sports, and politics.

To be sure, all wasn't always celebratory. In the nineteenth century, few cities in America were more hostile to Irish immigrants than Boston. And once the Irish became more settled, few communities were more hostile to Jewish immigrants than the Irish. And although the city was once the center of America's

abolitionist movement, a mere century later, "busing" in Boston became synony-
mous with racial upheaval.

But still.

Across New England, this sense of sweeping, significant history—uplifting, peculiar, riveting, shameful, complicated, impactful, inspiring—is at once as
real, permanent, and ever-present as woods and water, white steeples on town
greens, rolling hills and low stone walls. New England wears its history—proud
and soiled—like a hard-earned team jacket.

My own first vantage point on all this was from the edge of Boston Harbor,
where I grew up in the small seaside town of Winthrop. Although I haven't lived
there since I was eighteen, I still miss the ocean. Not the planes, though. There
was no open space to speak of; at just over one square mile in area, it's among
the smallest, most densely populated towns in Massachusetts, lying mere yards
from some of Logan International Airport's busiest runways. Settled in 1630,
it's named for John Winthrop, the second governor of the Massachusetts Bay
Colony. His youngest son, Deane Winthrop, bought a home there. It still stands,
and is today the oldest continuously occupied home in the United States. (In
elementary school, it represented the most boring, continuously assigned field
trip.) But that's New England's everyday relationship with history: Only yards
from a busy intersection and a small convenience store, a four-hundred-year-old
relic is still being used, shaken daily by passing traffic out front and passing jets
overhead, holding mere passing interest today for locals who mostly forget it's
even there.

But still.

In New England, these iconic physical things seem to come first to mind: old
houses, old barns, old churches, old taverns, old mills, old seaports. *Old* is often
fetishized here. You go to Florida for the sun and warmth. You go to New England
for the old and out-of-print. In Massachusetts, each city and town announces its
age right there on a road sign: "Entering Salem, Est. 1626." In terms of European
settlement, that's old; only six years after the Pilgrims landed in Plymouth. (And
sixty-six years before Salem started putting "witches" on trial.) Nearby, on Cape
Ann, Gloucester's "Entering" sign reads "1642," and the city bills itself as "America's Oldest Seaport." Relatively speaking, of course. To the Pawtucket people,
a branch of the Pennacook, which predate white settlement by thousands of
years, Gloucester is actually a pretty new seaport.

But still.

The pervasive history is fascinating all the same. These physical places matter. They're the outward, existing portals to the centuries of history behind them. The old mill towns across New England first harnessed the power of its mighty rivers and were the doorway to a new life for millions of immigrants. Storied seaports like Gloucester and New Bedford were the genesis of New England's rich maritime history, and the fishing families who made them famous crafted their own chapter of the American story. The hills and mountain ranges—from the western mountains of Maine into the White Mountains of New Hampshire across to Vermont's Green Mountains—are New England's wind-blasted, rocky rooftops. In their valleys lie farms where families still till that rocky soil and pasture herds of dairy cows. They're hardy places. Some hang on and hark back to an earlier era, while others hang on by reimagining the family farm and reinventing rural life. And the surrounding small towns with their grassy commons, cozy diners, general stores, and small stone libraries—those uniquely public spaces that still embrace an increasingly rare sense of kinship and community—are all sacred spaces. Rare, precious, and uplifting.

But still.

For all the powerful sense of place, purpose, and history that these iconic physical things convey, it's what's *behind* them, what *made* them, what still *tills* them, that matters more: the people. For over twenty-five years, my job as a journalist has been to tell the stories of New England. The places are easy to find. The stories and the people behind them take more effort. Farms and fishing boats don't talk. Farmers and fishermen and -women do. (Well, mostly.)

JERICHO CENTER COUNTRY STORE, VERMONT. (ART DONAHUE)

And those lovely little (and big) towns—Jericho, Harrisville, Sanford, Danbury, Putney—sure open up more after you've tried the homemade hash at the diner, or have struck up a friendly chat at the local general store about pretty much anything.

New Englanders have a reputation for being somewhat reserved and stand-offish. Tough to approach and not easy on strangers. True for the most part. (Especially Mainers.) But not entirely. Everyone—from Portland, Maine, to Portland, Oregon—has stories to tell. And in truth, everyone likes to be asked about them. Our stories define our lives for ourselves and distinguish our lives from others. We're proud of them. Or ashamed, amused, embarrassed. Or all of the above. But they're *our* stories. They're the individual threads of our experiences that, over time, weave together to form the fabric of a human life. They help us make sense of how our experiences have led us to where we are now. And hearing the stories of others helps us make sense of life as a whole, the human experience.

Granted, some stories aren't meant to be shared. And never are. (Despite coaxing.) Thankfully, over the years, many people *have* shared many of their stories with me. This book is full of them. (Even a few from Maine.) These are the most memorable people I've met in all of my New England travels. Their stories have stayed with me. Each one is a treat to recall. Their stories paint a region's still-living heart and its still-vibrant soul. Their achievements and creations speak to the region's timeless ingenuity. Their struggles speak to people—in New England and everywhere—who overcome and carry on, if only to claim a life of simple meaning, purpose, and dignity. And through it all, their unbowed, unfailing sense of humor captures the essence behind the old Mainer's response to the visitor's question: "Lived here all your life?"

"Not yet."

—⫷◆⫸—

AUTHOR'S NOTE

This book takes the form of a travelogue. Which, in its way, it is. Most of the places and people written about here were part of what was usually a weeklong trip for a story I was working on. But many of the places (and some of the people) were visited more than once over the years, often multiple times. So, rather than one, single, contiguous trip, the book is instead a composite of many trips. One narrative constant? Diners.

CAPITOL DINER, LYNN, MASSACHUSETTS.

Diners were first created in New England in the mid-nineteenth century to accommodate factory workers whose shifts ended at hours when most eateries were closed. The first ones were actual train cars pulled onto a siding and converted to serve food. Some say the first diner was in Worcester, Massachusetts; some say Woonsocket, Rhode Island. I say, why quibble? Is it not enough that this blessed thing came to be?

Throughout the book, diners are highlighted as sidebars. Diners are not only colorful, local landmarks in and of themselves, they're also local touchstones, literally offering a "taste" of a place. These living (surviving?) beacons of light and chrome, warmth and coziness, of coffee and community, are places I seek out and stop at on every single trip. If I'm lucky, I find a new one I haven't been to before. If I'm really lucky, I get to stop back in and see old friends who are (thankfully) keeping the home fires and home fries going for another year. In their own way, local diners, like local general stores (another routine stop), tell the stories of their cities and towns, as well as the people who live there. Why wouldn't they? Diners, like general stores, are natural gathering places. Sooner or later, everyone comes in. Diners are one of the best places to find good, local stories.

And if you're *really* lucky, some good homemade hash.

In its essence, travel is less about landscapes than about people—

not power brokers but pedestrians, in the long march of Everyman.

–Paul Theroux

CHAPTER 1

Old King's Highway:
Landfall, Land-Grabs, and Mini-Golf

Of all the made-up history surrounding the Pilgrims (no one knows if they ever stepped on a rock, never mind the chipped-up boulder that's displayed today), it's a lesser-known historical fact that would send shivers down the backs of New Englanders. The truth is, after more than two storm-tossed months at sea, when the *Mayflower* reached the shores of Cape Cod, it was also more than 200 miles northeast of the ship's intended destination: the mouth of the Hudson River. Forget Babe Ruth, Broadway, and Wall Street. New York almost had the Pilgrims, too.

Instead, the Nauset, a tribe of the larger Wampanoag Nation, got them.

Initially, the Pilgrims anchored in the protected harbor of present-day Provincetown ("P-town" to locals), and put a scouting party ashore in search of desperately needed food and water. The Hallmark image of the warm and fuzzy first Thanksgiving was still a ways off. Instead, on this early December morning in 1620, arrows and war cries flew from the trees near the shoreline, as a Nauset scouting party of its own tried to drive away the intruders.

Today, you can swim where once they skirmished. Driving along Route 6 in Eastham, you'll see a sign for "First Encounter Beach." You drive down Samoset Road, past ponds and salt marshes, eventually coming out to a small parking lot and a pretty, white-sand beach. And two dueling plaques on two big granite stones. One, placed in 1920, reads, "On this spot hostile Indians had their first encounter December 8, 1620 . . ." (the plaque lists the names of the *Mayflower*'s landing party). Nearby, another plaque, placed in 2001, reads, "Near this site, the Nauset Tribe of the Wampanoag Nation, seeking to protect themselves and their culture, had their first encounter . . ." The surf and the sky and the Atlantic Ocean there may look much the same as they looked four hundred years ago, but clearly views on the fateful "first encounter" have changed over time.

Route 6, also known as the Mid-Cape Highway, is the main east–west route on Cape Cod. It's generally thought of as the Cape's "main road," but it's actually just the last 100 miles or so of a cross-country highway that once extended more than 3,000 miles from Provincetown to Bishop, California. (California changed many of its highway numbers in the 1960s.) It's a fast route, and cars whiz along it. (Locals refer to one particularly accident-prone section as "Suicide Alley.")

Crossing onto the Cape over the Cape Cod Canal and the Sagamore Bridge, one can track the Cape's changing topography, as the Upper Cape's grass and short but sturdy hardwood trees give way to scrappy scrub pines in increasingly sandy soil. Through Brewster and Dennis, to the Cape's "elbow," the exits fly up quick; it's the most populated part of the Cape. But past Eastham and the beginning of the National Seashore, the landscape changes. The coastline just off Route 6 is protected, even if the small strip malls, souvenir stands, and seafood joints never entirely disappear from the roadside itself.

By Wellfleet and Truro and the advance to the Outer Cape, the landscape is open, flat, and punctuated only by low, rolling sand dunes. At points, the ocean is nearly visible from both sides of the shifting, sandy narrowness. Indeed, the National Seashore—the "Province Lands"—comprises over 8,000 acres between Chatham and Provincetown, and this tip of the Cape offers the most vivid sense of the windswept and barren natural beauty this area once was entirely. "Wild and desolate," is how Henry David Thoreau saw it during a visit in the mid-nineteenth century. He also saw the future. "The time must come when this coast will be a place of resort for those New Englanders who really wish to visit the sea-side," wrote Thoreau. "At present, it is wholly unknown to the fashionable world."

Today, it is wholly *known*, and properties on the Outer Cape (not to mention the offshore Cape Islands of Nantucket and Martha's Vineyard) sell for millions. Visitors pour over the Cape's two bridges, their cars clogging the approaches and exits every weekend from the end of May to mid-October, making "desolation" only a dream for the Cape's 230,000 or so year-round residents, who count the crowded days till fall, when the Cape—and their regular seat at the local coffee shop—will be theirs again.

I get it. As a kid, some of my best summer memories are of camping on the Cape, collecting driftwood, and playing in the surf at signature beaches like Nauset, Marconi, and Coast Guard. Nowadays, a Cape visit has far more appeal in early or late spring, fall, or even winter. Sure, the swimming's dicey (at least without a wet suit), but the crowds and the traffic are gone, and it's possible to simply have the space and breathing room to stand back and actually appreciate some of the natural beauty.

Skipping Route 6, Route 6A, also known as the "Old King's Highway," runs for about 62 miles, just to the north of and roughly parallel with Route 6, between the Upper Cape town of Bourne, to Orleans, at the "elbow." Route 6A is a slower route, and a genuinely meandering, two-lane, local road. One of only four National Scenic Byways in Massachusetts, it winds through historic bayside Cape towns like Sandwich, Yarmouth, Dennis, and Brewster, comprising the country's largest contiguous historic district. Towns like Sandwich have histories going back centuries and are quaint and lovely without being fake about it. On the other hand, the modern world is, alas, very much there; you'll find just about any national chain store you can think of all along the route, as well as an assortment of shopping plazas. Like miniature golf? It's very big on the Cape; you'll pass one course after another. Nautical themes—especially pirates and whales—are especially popular. Cape Cod is like the St. Andrews of mini-golf.

None of which was on my mind on a warm but cloudy early September day some years back. I was driving south on Route 3 out of Boston, which runs 40 miles or so past the city's South Shore, to Bourne on the Cape Cod Canal, then over the Sagamore Bridge where it connects to Route 6 and the Cape itself.

Route 3 South is also known as the Pilgrims Highway, which makes sense, as the highway slices through Plymouth, my first stop. In fact, the highway runs within just a couple of miles of the Pilgrims' original settlement.

The largest town area-wise in Massachusetts (nearly 100 square miles), Plymouth straddles Route 3, encompassing a large state forest on its inland side, and more than 20 miles of coastline along Cape Cod Bay on its ocean side. It likes to call itself "America's Hometown," and its downtown plays the part. Along its waterfront you'll find a replica of the *Mayflower*, as well as a columned, open-air monument, behind whose iron fencing lies a refrigerator-sized rock that the Pilgrims supposedly stepped on while coming ashore in 1620. Running just up the hill from the waterfront is Leyden Street, where some of the Pilgrims' first dwellings stood. On Main Street, at Speedwell Tavern, I wonder how many folks enjoying their chicken wings and beer know that it's named for the *Mayflower's* ill-fated sister ship, which sprang a leak, turned back to England, and never made it to the New World. (Making the *Speedwell* the Pete Best of ships.)

As a kid in the backseat, headed south on Route 3 to the Cape, I knew when I saw the "Plymouth" exit signs that we were almost there. Now, I think of the Pilgrims. I think of the sea-battered *Mayflower*, its soggy sails dripping in the winter hush, dropping anchor in the icy morning mist of Plymouth Harbor. I think of Native faces, warily peering from behind tall pines out to the water, beholding this spectral vision that has suddenly appeared in their midst.

Off the highway, I'm threading my way through a suburban neighborhood, to the end of a small cul-de-sac, where a few other cars are parked alongside what looks like an entrance into some woods. A group of ten or so people, young and older, are milling about; everyone has rakes and yard tools.

"You ready?" Melissa Harding-Ferretti shakes my hand and gestures toward the woods.

"Lead the way," I say with a smile.

Harding-Ferretti, a slim, long-haired woman with a quick laugh, is president of the Herring Pond Wampanoag Tribe, whose homelands extend from the Plymouth area to the Upper Cape itself.

"First, a quick smudging," she says, introducing me to Troy Currence, a tall and burly guy with a shaved head who is the tribal medicine man.

"It's about cleansing and spirituality, and open heart and good intentions," he says amiably.

Smudging is an ancient Native American ritual that uses the wisp of smoke to heighten spiritual awareness. For the Wampanoag, it's often done with pine smoldering in a small seashell. Currence briskly waves the smoking shell around my torso, my arms, my head, then pats me on the shoulder.

"There you go!"

With that, we're off on a narrow path through the woods.

"This was all private property," says Harding-Ferretti, juggling two long rakes, a big orange bucket in her hand bouncing with her stride. "So it was a place we were not allowed to go, even though it was part of our original reservation."

The path widens out to an opening—a huge ball field. Our party turns sharply to the right, back into the woods and up a hill; there's no defined path now. Another opening. It's a small grassy area, perhaps the size of a decent-sized backyard, surrounded by woods. In some places at the edges of the plot, remnants of a rusted, waist-high, wrought-iron fence pop up through the grass. It is, in fact, a plot. In a few spots where the grass has been cleared to the ground, several old gravestones lean at slight angles, the dirt at their bases freshly raked, as if the stones have only recently been revealed. Which they have been.

"The first time I walked up here, I had to go in through the ball field because I wasn't familiar with the paths," says Harding-Ferretti, now leaning on a rake as she surveys the scene. "It had been untouched then. But I could see the graves in the overgrown grass. I had to turn back after my tears and sort of say, 'I'll be back, we'll be back to help you.' And here we are."

The site is a former Wampanoag burial ground, dating back nearly two hundred years. The Herring Pond Tribe made it a mission to reclaim it, and honor these forgotten ancestors. In 2018, Plymouth town officials voted unanimously to deed back 6 acres to the tribe, including the former cemetery. Herring Pond members were thrilled, though as Harding-Ferretti points out, it was but a sliver of what was once theirs.

"This was part of the original reservation lands of the Herring Pond Wampanoag. It's where we had lived for thousands of years, but when the colonists arrived, they established this area as the Herring Pond Plantation, which at the time was almost a thousand acres."

On this early fall day, the work is about continuing to clear the former burial ground. Many of the volunteers are related. Troy Currence is joined by his daughter, Kendall, a junior at Northeastern University, where she is a star basketball player.

I had just finished chatting with Troy, when I catch her attention and step over.

"So, is he working you pretty hard today?" I ask, gesturing toward her dad.

The two share a laugh.

"Not too bad, no—he's harder on me at home." She grins, as her dad smiles and continues raking nearby. "Seriously, he's taught me so many things, and I mean to pass it on."

"Does the tribal identity still run deep among younger members, like you?" I ask her.

"For a lot of us, yes," she says, nodding. "I'm only twenty, but when I'm older and have kids of my own, yeah, pass it on to them, you know? You gotta keep it going."

People rake, they cut grass, some on their hands and knees trimming around the stones. There is the chatter of people sharing a task, catching up, and occasional bursts of laughter, all amid the steady snip-snip of pruning shears.

HERRING POND TRIBAL CEMETERY, PLYMOUTH, MASSACHUSETTS.

"These are our family members," says Troy Currence, waving his shears at a stone, pausing to wipe his brow with his shirt. "Even though we're raking leaves and cutting branches, we're also interacting with our loved ones."

Seven gravestones had been fully documented so far; Harding-Ferretti is certain there'll be more. She and I stand looking down at the smallest gravestone that had been documented.

"This is Lucy Anne," says Harding-Ferretti softly. She kneels down and brushes some dirt and green clippings off the stone's inscription. "According to the records, she died in 1831. She was three years old."

The raking and clipping continue as morning turns to early afternoon. Other gravestones and names, long lost to view, slowly reappear from the cleared brush. The most recent stone uncovered dates to 1857. An anthropologist is helping to document the findings. Eventually, the tribe hopes to clean up the rest of the 6 acres, perhaps create some walking trails.

"This will become part of our traditional ecological knowledge project," says Harding-Ferretti. "But it was so important for us to start with this plot. It's about restoring hallowed ground. We needed to honor these folks that are buried here, and who were neglected on this hilltop knoll for so, so long."

"This is a labor of love for you, for the tribe," I observe.

"Oh, absolutely. These are our ancestors. They're family. We owe them this."

A seagull's loud squawk above draws our gaze; I'm reminded how close the ocean is, even here by the woods.

MILL POND DINER
(Wareham, MA)

What may be the best diner on the Cape isn't actually on the Cape itself, but rather just over the Bourne Bridge on the mainland side in Wareham, which has long billed itself as "Gateway to Cape Cod." (More recently, the town has begun promoting a new slogan, "It's Better Before the Bridges.") The Mill Pond Diner, built in 1950 (Jerry O'Mahony Co. / Elizabeth, New Jersey), began life in Providence, Rhode Island, before being moved to its present location by the late William "Biff" Goyette, who owned and ran it for nearly forty years. It is every inch authentic: shiny stainless steel, cushy blue and yellow booths by the windows, counter stools set at the Formica counter exactly twenty-four inches on center. Locals love it, and why shouldn't they? It's open before six a.m., the menu checks off pretty much every diner basic (great BLT), prices are still on the lower side, and breakfast is served all day. (Not a big Eggs Benedict fan myself, but I did get a kick out of the "Eggs Ben And J. Lo" on the menu.) Given that the Cape itself lacks an authentic diner with the Mill Pond's history, perhaps the town of Wareham should tweak that new slogan: "It's Better Breakfast Before the Bridges."

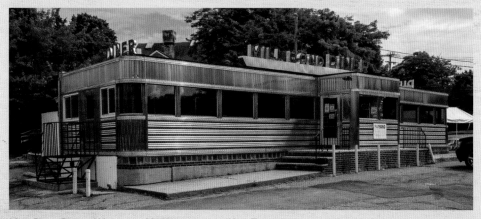

Mill Pond Diner, Wareham, Massachusetts. (Ken Zirkel)

A short while later, I'm back in my car, back on Route 3, continuing south. After about 15 miles or so, the Sagamore Bridge looms up. In summer tourist season, I'd be slowed to a crawl in what can be several miles of traffic backed up before the bridge. On this fall day, I fly by, up and over the canal, and onto Route 6 with the Cape laying out ahead of me for 63 miles. But I'm only going half that far. I exit at West Harwich, and in minutes I'm driving through still-green and leafy neighborhoods of tidy low-slung homes—"Capes." I've found the house; two kayaks on the roof of a car, and the sound of an electric sander coming from the garage.

"This is our happy place," says Pat Taylor, describing the garage in which a sleek, handmade, sixteen-foot wooden kayak is slowly taking shape. She laughs when I tell her that I knew I'd found the right place when I heard the sander. The sander, as it turns out, is one of the only electric tools they use.

"It's so nice to come out here and not have the power tools running, you know?" says soft-spoken Bill Witmer. "On a job site, you've got the saws and the hammers and the nail guns, you've got all this noise going on. But you come out here and it's peaceful, you know? You can just lose yourself."

Partners Taylor and Witmer know all about noisy work sites. As older adults with grown children, they met through their construction work for Habitat for Humanity, where Witmer was volunteering, and Taylor was a site supervisor. They both loved the Cape, and had a mutual affinity for kayaking and wooden boats in general.

"People really aren't used to seeing wooden kayaks—wooden anything any-more, right?" I ask Witmer, as he gently brushes some tiny wood shavings from the surface of the hull next to him, then leans down and blows away the dust that's left.

"No, it's a lost art. It really is. And that's sad, because they're beautiful things."

Three types of cedar are used for their wooden kayaks, which are the tradi-tional "Osprey" model, though Witmer and Taylor decorate each of theirs with an elaborate inlaid design that varies with each kayak they make. Even with the wood, it's astounding how light the kayak is—only forty-five pounds.

"It's like night and day when you're paddling a wooden one this light—there's no resistance in the water," says Witmer, adjusting his eyeglasses. "The plastic ones have wide hulls, they have to plow through the water; the wood ones are narrow and just glide through."

He invites me to hold one end and see for myself.

Bill Witmer.

"I cannot get over how light this is!" I exclaim, as Witmer and I gently lift each end from its supports in the garage, easily raising it up and down several inches.

"Amazing, isn't it?" He smiles.

They make just two of these kayaks a year. Each one requires about five hundred hours of labor to finish, all by hand at every step.

"Sometimes it's two hours out here, sometimes it's eight hours," says Taylor.

Their production pace has picked up over time; their first kayak took almost eight months to build.

"We've gotten fancier and we've gotten faster," says Witmer.

"We've also gotten older!" says Taylor, chuckling.

Both well into their seventies, the pair still loves to kayak as much as they can.

"The Herring River, other little rivers that we have here, it's such a beautiful area to paddle in," says Witmer.

Indeed, to be on one of the Cape's many small rivers and salt marshes at sundown on a beautiful summer evening, low on the water, tall green reeds and sea grass softly waving in the otherwise dusky stillness . . . that's the uniqueness of a kayak.

"I just love the peace and quiet and serenity," agrees Taylor. "We are blessed living here because of those little rivers we have to paddle in."

The couple is used to people stopping them, even on the water, to marvel at the beauty of the kayaks, and to ask where they got them. They love to be able to say, "Actually, we made them." One of their finished kayaks can sell for over five thousand dollars. But Taylor and Witmer also have an affinity for thinking of others and helping out in their community. It's not something new for either one of them. And it's personal. Both grew up without a lot of money; both know what it can feel like to go without things many take for granted. Like a warm and safe home.

"I was a single parent raising a daughter," says Taylor. "I would have definitely qualified for Habitat, had it been in the works at that point."

So, every year since 2005, one of the two kayaks the couple builds is donated to Habitat for Humanity of Cape Cod, and raffled off to raise money.

"It's an important way to make sure that other people have the opportunity for stability," continues Taylor. "Because the difference for kids when they move into their own home is absolutely amazing."

The couple's annual raffled handmade kayak has become a fund-raising mainstay for Habitat for Humanity on the Cape. That single kayak is frequently raffled off for the price of a new car, often raising over $30,000 to help build new homes for those who cannot afford to buy one.

"It won't build a whole house, but it'll buy a bunch of windows, maybe a couple of doors, you know, a few barrels of nails. That helps build a house," says Witmer, as he looks off through the windows of the garage for a moment. "When I was a kid, if I'd been lucky, I would have been living in a Habitat house. Where I lived when I was a kid, well, I don't want to see anyone do that today."

With that, the pair goes back to working on the new kayak.

It's late afternoon. There's still a long drive back. For a moment, off to the side, I watch Witmer and Taylor work. There's no chitchat, each intensely focused on

Finished kayak. (Habitat for Humanity of Cape Cod)

what they're doing. At moments, with no outward communication, one might look over at the other's work, and nod or give a thumbs-up. Witmer reaches over and passes a tool to Taylor. Without looking up, she grabs it and smiles.

"We know each other," Taylor says. "We check on each other, we make sure we're doing okay, but no need to just gab."

She slowly runs her hand over the sleek, finished cedar of the gleaming hull, looks over at Bill, then back to working intently on a section of the bow.

"But it's great," she says softly, taking a sip of water. "It's just great."

-⟨⟨⟨◆⟩⟩⟩-

It's dusk as I slip back onto Route 6 heading north. In thirty minutes or so, I'm back on Route 3, driving through Plymouth again, leaving the Cape farther and farther behind me. In 30 miles, the highway widens and the volume of cars whizzing along with me increases. I'm in Braintree, approaching the massive interchange of several highways better known locally as "The Split." I've reached the Boston metro area. From splits, to sloppy street layouts, to even sloppier signage, driving here is not for the faint of heart. But it's been a wonderful day, meeting some wonderful people who've made me feel a wee bit better about the world. That doesn't happen every day. But it did today.

(Loud car horn.)

And I refuse to let it be ruined at the end by a jerk with a missing headlight and a "Go Pats!" bumper sticker who just honked and gave me the finger for not moving over fast enough. Masshole.

(Deep breath.)

It's all good.

—◄◄◄◆►►►—

CHAPTER 2

Boston: Live Long and Prospah

"The Hub."

As nicknames go, at least it's logical. A look at a map proves it—huge concentric hoops of highways encircle the capital of Massachusetts, New England's largest city. Other nicknames—"Beantown," "Athens of America"—are just silly in comparison. Although, with a nod to the classics, Boston as Athens and New York as Sparta has always made some sense.

As American cities go, no question Boston is old. In 2030, the city will mark its four-hundredth anniversary. As always, though, age is relative; descendants of the Clovis People—ancestors of many modern North American tribes—might say "Congrats. Let us know when you celebrate your twelve-thousandth."

For all its vaunted history, Boston isn't even among the ten oldest US cities, although technically, it is considered slightly older than New York City. Which to many Bostonians is the only metric that matters.

I have plenty of childhood memories of the city: my first trip to Fenway Park (Sox lost 6-5 to the Orioles), boring field trips to the Museum of Science (made slightly less so by the eight-foot-tall Transparent Woman exhibit), and even more boring trips to Filene's Basement, where my mother or grandmother (or worse, both) would drag me as a boy while they shopped for underwear and shoes, rummaging through huge mark-down bins while I sat miserably on the floor. Later, I was less bored after copying more industrious and experienced kids, who knew to coil like a cat on the floor, ready to spring for the spare change that would invariably fall out of women's clothing while trying on bargain blouses and skirts in a frenzy. (There were no changing rooms in the Basement.)

In my early teens, I began to take the subway into the city. Boston Common was a magnet for young kids milling about, not necessarily making trouble, but enjoying the thrill of being on the periphery of trouble. Where once the colonial militia mustered and trained, where pirates and witches were once hung from "The Great Elm," now we just hung out. Created in 1634, the nation's oldest urban park to me was simply 50 acres abuzz with what little Winthrop lacked entirely: long-haired hippies, panhandlers, street musicians, and street people of all kinds. Couples danced, drinks were passed, drugs were sold, and always some half-crazy, half-dressed man or woman would be standing on a bench screaming something undecipherable at the top of their lungs. Even better, this whole colorful, urban scene played out essentially on the front lawn of the Massachusetts State House, whose classic white columns and iconic gold dome lent a lofty contrast to the gritty street scene below.

OLD STATE HOUSE, BOSTON.

In some ways, the close proximity between the workings of both the state, and the street, is perfectly Boston. Even in its early white-settler history, there was an arrogant, elevated element to original Puritan John Winthrop's vision of a "city upon a hill." Through the mid-nineteenth century, Lowells, Cabots, and Lodges remained the snooty, stodgy backbone of Boston's cultural and political life. As the old saying went:

And this is good old Boston,

The home of the bean and the cod,

Where the Lowells speak only to Cabots,

And the Cabots speak only to God.

Later, the Irish moved in, followed by succeeding waves of the "great unwashed" from all over Europe. By the twentieth century, Boston's increasingly outnumbered and outraged gentry were more and more confined to their Beacon Hill brownstones, there to find solace from the slovenly, to sip their sherry, clutch their pearls, commiserate among equals, and reminisce about an earlier golden age, when the city was theirs, pedigrees mattered, and all these stubby, swarthy, sweaty newcomers were still back in the barrio somewhere. Wherever the goddamn hell in the world that was.

Surely, the Wampanoag, spying the *Mayflower*, had once felt the same way about their own exclusive seaside neighborhood; watching those bedraggled strangers in their moldy woolens washing ashore and acting like they lived there.

Change came to an insular, stuffy city. It was about time. The starchy "city on a hill" took on real-life roots down on the less prosaic streets. Over time, the irony was that—as with most cities—the city's newer arrivals and non-whites tended to also settle among themselves, creating their own insular enclaves: the Irish in South Boston and Charlestown, the Italians in the North End and East Boston, the Chinese in what became "Chinatown," Blacks largely in Roxbury, Eastern European Jews in the West End, and so forth. And that's what Boston became and mostly still is: a city of separate neighborhoods, with separate cultures, separate outlooks, and separate grievances.

Not that a visitor to Boston is lost among a Balkan-like patchwork of far-flung neighborhoods. Physically, the city is relatively small and compact to begin with. Its land area—48.4 square miles—makes it the second-smallest major American city. (San Francisco has 47 square miles.) Like San Francisco, it sits on a large bay, its small size making it easily and entirely walkable. Considering that the city lacks a definitive street grid layout, and signage is notoriously lousy (not to mention its notoriously lousy drivers), walking is one of the best and safest ways to get around Boston. In less than thirty minutes, it's possible to walk (briskly) from one end of the city, at the waterfront, all the way west to the other end, to Fenway Park and the bordering town of Brookline.

It took twenty years (and would ultimately cost more than $22 billion), but by 2007, Boston had finally removed (and depressed underground) its eyesore of an elevated highway that, since the early 1960s, had paralleled—and obscured—the waterfront. Where the ugly highway hulked, the Rose Kennedy Greenway—a 1.5-mile stretch of linear public parks—has reconnected the waterfront with the city.

Away from Boston's downtown, the city's neighborhoods over the decades have changed and evolved as well. The change there is most evident not in buildings and roads, but people. In East Boston's Maverick Square, for example, the once largely Irish and Italian-American ethnic profile has shifted over time to largely Latino, with significant newer arrivals of Asian, North African, East African, Turkish, and Arab populations.

Whole *new* neighborhoods have emerged, too. In just the first two decades of the twenty-first century, Boston's Seaport District on the South Boston waterfront has emerged as an entire mini-city, sprouting gleaming new highrises, trendy shops, and restaurants, all at an astonishing rate of development. Meanwhile, in many of the city's older working-class neighborhoods, as with older urban neighborhoods everywhere, life goes on without the glam and the gleam and the development. Issues around safety, jobs, education, transportation, and affordable housing continue to bedevil Boston's minority communities. Some things don't change. Some things don't get billions.

But only one major Boston neighborhood exists today only as a still life, only in photos, and only in memory. The city's legendary West End neighborhood was deliberately demolished and wiped from the map.

Geographically, the West End was bordered by the Charles River, the North End, Beacon Hill, and the heart of historic downtown Boston. It had long figured in the city's history; guiding lights of the American Revolution had lived there. In the early nineteenth century it had become home to many of the city's African Americans, and the famed African Meeting House on the south slope of Beacon Hill—once the center of the abolitionist movement—was separated from the West End only by Cambridge Street.

During succeeding waves of immigration in the later nineteenth century, the West End drew new residents from literally all over the world, especially Irish, Italians, and European Jews, as well as Greeks and Middle Easterners. By the twentieth century, it had become the city's most vibrantly diverse neighborhood. Thoroughly working-class, the West End was a warren of narrow streets, small shops, and tenement buildings. Those who lived there would recall later

WEST END STREET SCENE, 1950S. (THE WEST END MUSEUM)

how much they loved it. "The greatest neighborhood this side of heaven," was a famous description by a longtime resident.

By 1950, the West End was home to just under fifteen thousand people. One of them was a young Jewish kid named Leonard Nimoy.

"It really was a village," Nimoy recalled for the Yiddish Book Center's Wexler Oral History Project in 2010. The second son of Russian immigrants, Nimoy grew up in a West End tenement, sold newspapers as a teen in downtown Boston, and even seventy years later, still seemed to marvel at the workaday diversity of his boyhood neighborhood.

"We had an iceman who'd put a block of ice on his shoulder and come up the two or three flights. He was an Italian who spoke Yiddish because he had so many Jewish customers. It was that kind of a cross-over relationship—the Italians spoke Yiddish, the Jews spoke Italian—my friends were a mix of Jews and Italians, the second floor was Italians, the third floor was Jewish."

Nimoy, who left the West End in 1949 to seek an acting career in California, later became world-famous as "Mr. Spock" on the legendary TV series, *Star Trek*. But by the time the USS *Enterprise* was making its first foray toward faraway galaxies, it was Nimoy's beloved neighborhood back on Earth that had been vaporized. In the 1950s, the view by many *outside* the West End was that the neighborhood, thriving and diverse as it was, was nonetheless a "slum."

LEONARD NIMOY WITH DAUGHTER JULIE, CALIFORNIA, 2014. (JULIE NIMOY)

What many of these well-to-do onlookers (most of whom had no connection with the West End) really saw was not so much a slum, but a low-income, hardscrabble section of the city that possessed little political power but did have huge development potential. The Housing Act of 1949 had made massive federal funding available for what was then called "urban renewal." Add in a pliant mayor and a Boston Redevelopment Authority itching to, well, redevelop, and the mix was irresistible. In 1958, seven thousand West End residents and families were displaced by eminent domain and forced to move. Forty-six acres were razed to the ground. A tight-knit, colorful, and extraordinarily diverse neighborhood whose history stretched back centuries seemed to vanish overnight in a huge cloud of dust. Gone.

In its place now towered five luxury high-rises. The familiar and cluttered landscape of small shops and tenements gave way to wide, antiseptic thoroughfares, bordered by equally wide and antiseptic shopping centers and parking lots. Leonard Nimoy's "village" was no more. No one needed to know another language now. There was no one left on the streets to talk to.

For a visitor without knowledge of this history, the West End today makes little impression at all. One might be going to Massachusetts General Hospital or headed to some other business in the area. There are some eateries, there's plenty of parking. It's a boring streetscape with little pedestrian traffic other than on busy Cambridge Street

WEST END RAZED, C. 1960. (THE WEST END MUSEUM)

alongside Beacon Hill. There is little life at all; it's not a neighborhood.

One entire block of the West End is occupied by a state property, the Lindemann Mental Health Center, a massive concrete structure in the "Brutalist" style that is so cold, forbidding, and stunningly ugly that a nearby parking garage looks open and inviting by comparison. A few blocks past Massachusetts General Hospital, in the permanent shade of a busy highway overpass, lies a long, curving concrete wall. On it, in big inset letters, is inscribed THE GREATEST NEIGHBORHOOD THIS SIDE OF HEAVEN. It's one of

THE WEST END'S SINGLE SURVIVING TENEMENT, BOSTON, MASSACHUSETTS.

the few visible references in the West End that mark and memorialize the real neighborhood that once existed there.

"That's where his house was, just past the loading dock, on the other side of that building."

I'm standing on Blossom Street on an early fall day with Tom Stocker, an accomplished Boston painter. He's pointing out where Leonard Nimoy's childhood home stood, a three-story tenement on Chambers Street. The building, and the street, are long gone. Blossom Street survives. A block away is MGH (Mass General Hospital). In front of us, on the opposite side of the street, are two of the few surviving buildings of the original West End. One is the Winchell Elementary School, built in 1884, now owned and used as work space by MGH. Next to the school is the more famous and significant West End House. It was built in 1929 as a gathering place for young Jewish immigrants, offering language classes, and athletic and social programs.

"The West End House, Tom—Nimoy spent a lot of time there, yes?"

"Oh, yes, he was there for all sorts of activities, lectures, drama; he played basketball there."

"Is it safe to say," I ask, "that the West End neighborhood was really a guiding influence throughout Leonard Nimoy's life?"

"Absolutely. He never forgot his roots here. He loved the fact that it was a polyglot neighborhood, people from everywhere. He loved that, and he never forgot it."

Tom Stocker is a gentle, seventy-something man with a quick laugh and gray wispy hair, with corresponding goatee. He looks professorial and walks with a cane. He's a wonderfully talented artist who's perfected a kind of pointillism in his trademark works. The pieces are fascinating and time-consuming to create, but they don't take all of his time these days. A large chunk of his non-working time is actually devoted to Leonard Nimoy. He's not a Trekkie, was never even a big fan of *Star Trek*. But he's become something of an authority on Spock.

TOM STOCKER, WEST END, BOSTON.

"He was the 'other,' and a lot of people identified with him because of that. Because he was different, he was the visitor, he didn't always know how to relate with the other inhabitants of the *Enterprise*, and they often didn't know how to relate to him," says Stocker in the quiet of his South End studio. "That 'otherness' is something that many people relate to in many different ways."

Stocker also relates to Nimoy on a more personal level. "I really do feel a connection. Maybe it's because of the way we grew up, in the neighborhoods that we grew up in. And his love for humanity."

Stocker's interest in Nimoy happened by chance. After the actor's death in 2015, Stocker saw a documentary about Nimoy, produced by his son, Adam. In the film, father and son returned to Boston, and the West End. The sense of deep emotional connection, and loss, is palpable, and powerful. So is Nimoy's love for the city of his youth. Which, as Stocker learned, was something that animated Nimoy his entire life.

"Boston shaped his character. He encapsulates the hometown-boy-makes-good, but he never forgets Boston," says Stocker softly, his voice cracking slightly. "He comes back. He loved Boston. He comes back. Again and again. He's always there for the city."

All during Nimoy's working years in California, he continued to help support many organizations back in Boston, frequently returning for events at the city's Boys and Girls Club, and his beloved West End House. He and his wife, actress Susan Bay, created a foundation for the arts and awarded millions in grants to more than fifteen different institutions in Boston, Cambridge, and elsewhere in Massachusetts.

What bothered Tom Stocker was that Nimoy's hometown had never publicly expressed its gratitude and love for its native son. And he thought it was high time. "He ventured out west, but never stopped loving his hometown. And I felt that should be recognized."

So in 2015, by himself, Stocker started the Leonard Nimoy Memorial Project. He was its sole member.

"First, I just thought in terms of, well, if there were a memorial, what would it look like? Should it be Leonard Nimoy the man? Or should it be Mr. Spock? Then I thought, well, maybe a hologram, but life-size. And I found somebody at MIT who was anxious to do something like that, but then it turned out that one of the complications of having a hologram was that it would need to be housed in a building."

"And you felt strongly," I ask Stocker, "that however it turned out, it had to be outside and accessible to everyone, yes?"

"Yes. In my mind, it had to be outside, *had* to be."

Ultimately, for the fundamental question of what it should look like, it was as if Spock himself reached out. Stocker smiles and raises both hands wide, his fingers flashing the message of Spock's iconic Vulcan greeting–*Live long and prosper.*

"It just hit me–that's it!" Stocker gleefully exclaims. "And the idea locked in."

Stocker still needed a skilled artist to craft the idea into a sculpture, not to mention a place to put it. He'd been impressed by the work of accomplished sculptor David Phillips, so he approached him about his vision for the Nimoy project.

" 'Course, I didn't know who Tom was," smiles Phillips, a genial older fellow with a shock of graying hair and a similarly speckled beard. "But I thought, yeah, that hand gesture–'Live long and prosper'–it's a great universal symbol in a way. I thought it could work."

And with that, Phillips was on board. It was understood that full funding, needless to say, would need to materialize in order to create a full sculpture, but Phillips set about drawing up some sketches. In his light and airy Cape Cod studio overlooking a small pond in Sandwich, Phillips points out several scaled-down maquettes of his own vision, each encompassing what would be a large translucent hand making the Vulcan greeting, seeming to glow from the inside. It's a very large hand; tiny model onlookers are dwarfed next to it.

"Three-plus times taller than we are," says Phillips. "But I think it needs a monumental scale to get it across. I don't think you'd want a small one. So, I'm thinking big at this point!"

As of 2023, things were moving along far further than Stocker had allowed himself to hope. For a prolonged period, the COVID-19 pandemic, the Ukraine

LEONARD NIMOY MEMORIAL, BOSTON (ARTIST'S RENDERING). (BOSTON MUSEUM OF SCIENCE)

War, and inflation all made fund-raising extremely difficult. But in the midst of it all, Boston's venerable Museum of Science announced that it would not only help raise funds for the memorial, but would also provide a permanent location for it on the grounds of the museum.

"It's a great symbol for a positive vision of humanity," says museum president Tim Ritchie. "Our mission is to inspire a lifelong love of science. We're not a backward-looking museum, we're a forward-looking museum. *Star Trek* is always looking forward, and it gets people seeing themselves in science."

More than ever these days, Tom Stocker is looking forward, too. He's thrilled with the symbolism of the proposed site itself. The Science Museum's front lawn directly faces the West End, just a few blocks away. He continues to tirelessly lead the fund-raising efforts, and sees the Vulcan greeting in his sleep, as he turns out hand-painted postcard after postcard of it to attract donors. For nearly a decade, he's been the founding visionary and lead ambassador for a project that has yet to be fully realized. He has refused to take a dime.

As he sits in his studio, dipping his small brush and sketching the Vulcan greeting in royal blue on a postcard, I ask him what it is that still drives him, still moves him forward every day, all for a memorial that has yet to be built, all for a man he never met.

"Well, I thought it was right. At this stage of my life, I have the time to do it, and over the past several years it's really become a part of me." He holds the brush still for a moment, slowly fingering it in his hand. "And at this stage, I guess there's also a part of me that really wants to do something, something that I can say, I helped do that. You know?"

These days, when I'm driving in Boston, especially passing by the West End, I think of Leonard Nimoy, and I think of Tom Stocker, too. Two passionately creative sons of this complicated city. Strangers, who will be forever connected here. Each with long lives, each having prospered, in their own different, wonderful ways.

DELUXE TOWN DINER

(Watertown, MA)

DELUXE TOWN DINER, WATERTOWN, MASSACHUSETTS.

Like most major American cities (especially in the Northeast), downtown Boston once had a bunch of classic diners. Like most cities, most of those diners are memories now. (I still miss East Boston's Neptune Diner.) Landscapes change. (Though sometimes things reappear; the century-old South End landmark, Charlie's Sandwich Shoppe, in the original 1927 building, is enjoying a new lease on life.)

In neighboring Watertown, however, the venerable Deluxe Town Diner on Mt. Auburn Street endures. Unlike most classic diners, it was built in the 1940s on its original site, not prefabricated by a manufacturer. (The present diner actually enlarged an original, smaller Worcester diner that stood there.) Today, with its distinctive glass-block windows and two-tone colors, it continues to command its corner on Mt. Auburn Street, where it is beloved by both locals and legions of fans from afar. In 1999, it was added to the National Register of Historic Places. No mystery why. It is the essence of a cozy, homey, and inviting diner where regular and newcomer alike are inclined to take a breath and stifle a smile on sitting down. It feels that friendly.

Daryl and Don Levy seem as much like den parents as diner owners. Daryl often refers to it as the "people's diner."

"It definitely is," she smiles. "When a new family moves into the area and comes in, I say, 'This is *your* diner.' We just love to share it with however many people we can."

'Course, it helps that they've created a menu that has all the classics (blue plate specials), but also some nice, newer touches, too. The pancakes are legendary. "Some people tell us, if they were away," says Daryl, "the first thing they do when they get back is head for the diner for pancakes. We like to think they're some of the best around."

So is the diner they're served in.

CHAPTER 3

Up the North Shore, and a Detour to the "Other" Cape

Through the tunnel, into East Boston, past Logan Airport, Route 1A winds along close to the water. For several miles past East Boston, it passes through the city of Revere, paralleling Revere Beach Boulevard. Over 3 miles long, Revere Beach was officially opened under state management in 1896, becoming America's first public beach. Only minutes from the city and accessible by public transportation, it became instantly popular. Alas, its popularity was also its undoing. Over the next sixty or so years, it became lined with cheap bars and pizza joints, though families and kids (including me) also flocked to its arcades and amusements, including what was, for a time, the largest wooden roller coaster ever built. By the 1980s, it all came down. Today pricey condos and apartment towers stand where the bars and amusements once were. The beach itself has returned to the simpler outdoor recreation it represented in its heyday.

REVERE BEACH, MASSACHUSETTS.

Also in the beach's heyday was a storied narrow-gauge railroad that ran by the entire shoreline. The Boston, Revere Beach and Lynn Railroad opened in 1875, running from the North Shore city of Lynn, through Revere, to East Boston, where passengers could take a ferry across the harbor to Boston's waterfront. It was a thirty-minute, twenty-cent ride from Lynn to East Boston, which made the line both convenient and affordable. Once described as "the narrow gauge with wide appeal," its most popular stop was at Revere Beach, where thousands of passengers—towels, umbrellas, and picnic baskets in hand—would disembark on a hot summer day. Like Rockaway and Brighton Beaches in New York, free, public, urban beaches were, and still are, literal oases from the city heat. By 1914, more than seven million passengers a year were using the BRB&L, making it for a time the nation's most commercially successful line of its type.

Over the next couple of decades, with the growth of automobiles and the opening of Boston's Sumner Tunnel, the Boston, Revere Beach and Lynn Railroad rapidly lost ridership, and ceased running entirely by 1940. Today, an aboveground section of the MBTA (Massachusetts Bay Transportation Authority) Blue Line runs through Revere over the same right-of-way where the old BRB&L once ran. The history still pops up in unexpected ways.

"When my son was born seventeen years ago," says Todd Gieg, "We were living in the Fort Point Channel area of Boston, and I had been photographing along Revere Beach. It was one of my favorite areas to photograph. Oh—and we were moving to Lynn!"

Gieg, a slight, sixty-something former photographer with thick glasses, a quick laugh, and a warm, engaging energy sits back for a moment, the better to take in how utterly unlikely and yet perfectly ordered is the track his own life has taken.

"I decided when my son was born that I would get out my American Flyer trains and make him a railroad. I was going to call it the 'Fort Point, Revere Beach and Lynn.' Then I bought a model kit, and the directions referred to the 'Boston, Revere Beach and Lynn Railroad.' I couldn't believe it. That was essentially the name of the railroad I was going to build. I didn't know it existed. I decided I was fated to build it."

In 2007, when his son Max was five, Gieg began creating a 1/87th-scale model diorama of the Boston, Revere Beach and Lynn Railroad. It would be an immense project, and Gieg intended the model to be executed with painstakingly wrought accuracy and detail—even though he'd never built a model before.

"It began with fits and starts," Gieg tells me in 2019, during my first visit to his studio in a converted Lynn mill building. "I had a lot to learn about modeling, and I knew nothing about the railroads. So there was an enormous amount of research. I had to go to libraries, historical societies; I had to go on eBay and look for items that might be of use to me. I had to find at least *some* people who actually remembered the railroad."

"Did you find some?" I ask.

"I found a gentleman who used to jump into the water with his friends when the train would be coming across the trestle. They'd see who could stay there the longest."

Slowly, Gieg began incorporating the decades of history behind the railroad and the area it ran through. He set the landscape for the year 1895.

"It's before the invention of the automobile. Certain buildings that I love, like the Strathmore Hotel, burned down in 1896, which is also when the tracks themselves were moved off the beach, so it seemed to be the right year."

To get every tiny detail perfect, Gieg approached the level of research like a doctoral candidate.

"I got started very slowly, the research. Now I'm up to speed. I used to feel like there was a switch, and when the switch was on, I had limitless energy for the diorama. When it got switched off, though, I sometimes walked away from it for months."

"And now?" I ask.

"Now the switch is always on. Even when I'm not working on it, I'm thinking about it."

It is hard to fully describe what Gieg has been creating. It's not simply the size of it, which is large. He's building the diorama in six-foot-long, table-height modules. He estimates that, even compressing it somewhat, there will ultimately be up to ten of these modules to cover the geographic length of the railroad.

"If I didn't compress it, even though I'm at small-scale, the diorama would be over four hundred feet long."

Todd Gieg.

What's most stunning, though, is the almost mesmerizing detail. I found myself leaning into sections of the model—an entire trackside Lynn neighborhood, for instance, or a long-gone beachside hotel—peering in closer and closer, wondering where the detail would end. Speck-sized people peering back from behind third-floor windows . . . a hotel veranda, with dot-sized "real" oysters on "real" hotel china, surrounded by nearly microscopic utensils.

"Did you spot the guy taking a leak behind the building yet?" says Gieg, laughing.

Further south on the diorama, to Beachmont and Revere, inlets along the shore are dotted with small boats, buoys, and fishing shacks, on whose weathered roofs tiny seagulls perch, surveying the scene. A ball field abuts the railroad tracks, replete with players; a bandstand in a park sits near a sprawling resort hotel.

Needless to say, it takes a lot of time to create that level of detail for a diorama that will ultimately be as long as forty feet. And Todd Gieg has taken it. When we first met, he'd already been at work on the project for nearly twelve years. I visited him again in 2021, when he estimated it would take another eight or so years to finish.

Spain's Sagrada Familia came to mind.

"Thing is, when I began this, I was building it essentially for myself, my son. And I'm still building it for myself in a way. But over time, I've realized that I really want to share this."

After all, when Gieg began the project, his son, Max, was a little boy. He's now out of college. Things change. One man's solitary project has drawn the attention of other people. The Lynn Museum, founded in 1897 and today the anchor of the city's Arts & Cultural District, has committed to a permanent display for the diorama. Several of the finished modules have already been installed at the museum, often leaving young schoolkids in awe. (And, after a little too much awe early on, leaving them now on the other side of a protective Plexiglas barrier.)

"At first it was hard to let go of what I'd built," Gieg concedes. "But all I needed to do was remind myself that I don't want to keep this. The satisfaction would not be there. What I want is to share this. I love this area, I love sharing with people what was once here, especially kids."

Watching Gieg as he stops to intently peruse an old map or some period photos, or uses tweezers to arrange a tiny figure on a dock, or a small hair dryer to fluff up a patch of "grass" (a mix of ingredients he's concocted), I'm struck by an irony. He has devoted the last decades of his working life to preserving a small and authentic slice of New England history. Yet in his determination to get up and work every day, to cultivate something that will take years and years to fully blossom, he is *himself* something quintessentially New England: hardworking, wry, ingenious, creative, innovative, all with an abiding sense of his own place in the long history he's part of.

"I'm curious," I wonder, as he pauses to sip some water, "how much do you think about this project still going on, still taking years more, ending up taking, what—maybe *twenty years* by the time you're all done?"

He puts the glass down, inhales, looks across a section of what he's been working on.

"I'm sixty-six; my eyesight's not a guarantee, my ability to manipulate small things, my dexterity is not a given as I get older. I feel like I'm on a set amount of time to get this project completed. And that's always on my mind."

"Do you still enjoy it every day?" I ask. "Has the passion waned at all over time?"

He grins slightly, nods, rubs his chin.

"In the past, I've had moments where I'm thinking, this is going to take eight more years; am I going to be able to maintain my energy and enthusiasm? And sometimes I have a drought for a bit. But it always ends. I no longer have fear that I won't be able to finish it."

"You're in this to the end."

"Now I will cry," Gieg says, shaking his head. "You know, you hear people talk about the end of their lives, looking back, wishing that they had appreciated it more in the moment. For me, this project keeps me in the moment. It's exactly where I want to be all of the time. And I'm so grateful for that."

—◆—

Route 128 North (also known as the Yankee Division Highway) puts you on a 20-mile straight shot for Land's End on Massachusetts' "other" cape: Cape Ann. Through Danvers and Beverly, the extensive retail development all along the highway begins to dwindle, gone entirely by Manchester.

KELLY'S

(Revere, MA)

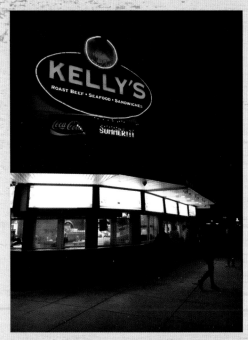

KELLY'S, REVERE BEACH, MASSACHUSETTS.

I can't recall the first time I was at Kelly's. Which makes sense, as I was a toddler. My dad had likely pulled over to grab a roast beef sandwich, feeding me a few french fries in the front seat while we drove home. As for the *last* time I was there, couldn't have been too long ago, as I'll routinely detour over there if I'm anywhere within 10 miles or so of Revere, Massachusetts. Which is where, about halfway up Revere Beach boulevard, Kelly's Roast Beef has been a landmark since 1951. Nothing fancy going on, then or now. It's the exact same corner walk-up place: order at one of several windows, wait, have your name called, then back to your car, or better, dine al fresco. Which, in Kelly's case, means simply crossing the street and finding a bench under the covered, century-old pavilion at the edge of Revere Beach. The heaping roast beef sandwiches on a sesame roll dripping with Kelly's special sauce are the go-to order. But the shore food—clams, scallops, fish and chips—are all really good, too. On a weekend day, the lines at all of the order windows can back up big-time. (I've been by at 9 p.m. on a late-fall weeknight and still found myself waiting in a short line.) For sure, Kelly's has become that dreaded thing for an eatery: a local institution. In the 1980s and '90s, they expanded to several other locations, though the original Revere one remains the only one on the ocean and, to its older, die-hard regulars, the only location they think of as "Kelly's." "How can it possibly taste the same," my dad wondered, "if you're not smelling stale suntan lotion and dodging seagull shit?"

(Oops—"Manchester-By-The-Sea."*) Huge rocks, mostly granite, poke out through the dense trees on both sides. There's much more of it to come.

Exits flash by: Route 133, Essex, Ipswich. For New Englanders, these are names that instantly conjure clams, boats, beach plum, tidal marshes, and salty ocean air. In summer, it's all of that. And some truly unique baseball, too. These are towns that are part of Cape Ann's Intertown Twilight League, recognized by Major League Baseball's Hall of Fame as the nation's oldest, active amateur baseball league. For someone who loves baseball, the ocean, and fried clams (Cape Ann's signature dish), it's a higher level of sublime thrill to sit and watch a ball game in the six o'clock golden-hour light of a summer evening, the Rockport Townies battling the home-team Essex Mariners, on a green and dusty diamond where only the stand of lush green trees and a slight rise in center field block a view of the ocean beyond. But nothing blocks the onshore breeze and the whiff of ocean air wafting in above the trees. (Prompting the Rockport coach to remind his hitters, "Wind's blowing in—keep the ball down, make 'em field it!")

In right field, however, there's an even more pronounced hill running up from the foul line, and thankfully, nothing to obscure the view of the fascinating building that crowns the hilltop. What looks like a sprawling Shingle Style private mansion of wood and fieldstone is actually entirely public. Built in 1893, it houses both the Essex Town Hall and the public library. I walked up the hill, keeping one eye on the game and the other on the building. As I walked around it, admiring it, I noted that it's listed on the US National Register of Historic Places. I also took note of some screaming foul balls, a couple of which landed mere feet from the building. National protection aside, I thought, with a wind blowing *out*, surely this building must take some direct hits.

I was right.

LIBRARY IN THE OUTFIELD, ESSEX, MASSACHUSETTS.

*In 1989, in a close town meeting vote, Manchester, Massachusetts, officially changed the town's name to "Manchester-By-The-Sea." The stated reason for the change was to avoid any confusion with the city of Manchester, New Hampshire, some 60 miles to the north. But that would be like confusing an older, slightly dinged-up Chevy Malibu with a brand-new, luxury Land Rover. Many think the name change had more to do with making an official distinction between a hardscrabble, blue-collar former mill town and the highly affluent, sailing and polo-playing town well south of it. By the sea—not the mills.

A few months after that summer twilight game, I was back in Essex and inside the library for a book talk I was giving. I asked library director Deborah French if balls from the games ever hit the building. She laughed. Loudly. But not like it was funny.

"Many a Monday morning I come in and there's a baseball in the room," she said, gesturing over toward the row of windows facing the ball field. "Well, that was before we had the new screens."

"Who gets billed for that?"

"I tried the league, but umm, no."

Good thing for the league, French is a baseball fan. She loves whatever it is that gets folks into the library. Even if it's a ball game outside the door.

"It's great when baseball season starts. You hear the bat, you hear folks cheering, kids'll come in and get books while their parents are watching the game. It's nice. It's all part of the community."

Through Ipswich, Essex, Manchester (by-the-whatever), and then, by West Gloucester, and, finally, water. Crossing over the A. Piatt Andrew Bridge, what many may think is the ocean below is actually the mouth of the Annisquam River, feeding its way into Gloucester Harbor. Until 1950, when the bridge was completed, the outer tip of Cape Ann had been an island. No more. Although there are times in summer when residents of Rockport and Gloucester may wish it still was.

Off the bridge, around the always-entertaining Grant Circle rotary (Massachusetts sprouts rotaries like Iowa sprouts corn), onto Route 127 North, and a 6.5-mile drive up to Cape Ann's northernmost tip. Winding through Annisquam, with Ipswich Bay on the left and its small inlets—Hodgkin's Cove, Plum Cove, Lanes Cove—reaching nearly up to the road as it winds by. Passing through the center of lovely little Lanesville and its tiny post office with the bright red doors. And all the while, the ocean only a block away on your left, playing hide-and-seek between the small shops and the old, two-story, wood-frame houses as you drive by. Many of these small houses were lived in by skilled stonecutters and quarry workers who once made Rockport world-famous.

"You go around in Rockport, look in certain yards, you'll see some granite that was carved by these guys; just amazing stuff."

In Rockport's Pigeon Cove, it's a brilliantly bright early April morning at Halibut Point. It's my favorite place on Cape Ann, and one of the most physically stunning spots in New England. I'm standing on a wide but flat rocky ledge overlooking the open ocean with Paul St. Germain, a Cape Ann historian and author. Despite the sun, the chill breeze in off the water ripples our jackets and makes it feel like late fall. The sky's an endless blue, the Atlantic a deep, roiling green. The churning surf far below us explodes against the dark gray rocks in rhythmic booms and bursts of white spray. The granite all around us has mostly aged to a speckled khaki color. There's a lot of it, even after so much was hammered, hacked, blown off, and carted away. The entire landmass of Cape Ann itself is a deep, massive, four-hundred-million-year-old granite outcropping that has supported vegetation on its surface. And for a time, it supported a huge granite industry. By the mid-nineteenth century, more than thirty quarries were thriving in Rockport, employing more than eight hundred thousand people.

The biggest was right here: Babson Farm Quarry, which drew immigrant quarrymen—particularly Irish, Finns, Swedes—to work Rockport's prized granite and to help feed the world's growing demand for it. As fast as it could be blasted and cut, it was being dragged by oxen to the shoreline, loaded onto ships, and sent off to help build landmarks like the Brooklyn Bridge and Holland Tunnel in New York, and Boston's Longfellow Bridge and Custom House Tower. Paving stones cut from Rockport granite lined streets in Paris and Havana, Philadelphia, and San Francisco. Alas, by 1929, with the Great Depression and the advent of concrete, the granite industry collapsed. The glory days here were gone.

FILLED-IN GRANITE QUARRY, HALIBUT POINT, ROCKPORT, MASSACHUSETTS. (MARK KANEGIS)

Up the North Shore, and a Detour to the "Other" Cape   33

Paul St. Germain and I have walked down to what was the main Babson quarry. We're standing on its rocky rim, some short scrub pines at our backs. From this perch, beyond the quarry in the foreground, there's a 180-degree panoramic view of the ocean. On a clear day, you can see out to southern Maine and New Hampshire's Isles of Shoals. In front and below us, the original, abandoned quarry itself looks like an enormous rock lagoon. The main pit is sixty feet deep, filled now with mostly freshwater that was once daily and heroically kept out.

"They kept a steam-driven pump running day and night to keep the water out, and to keep it semi-dry for themselves," says St. Germain.

"Big derricks, hauling out huge slabs, workers hanging on ropes," I recall from period photos I've seen. "Man, that had to be tough work year-round."

"Very dangerous work," St. Germain says, shaking his head. "No safety rules to speak of, no goggles, no masks, just raw hands, often not even gloves."

From the quarry, you can walk about half a mile down a path to the ocean's edge. Huge granite slabs—"castoffs"—are everywhere. People aren't. You can walk along the rocks and see nothing but circling seagulls, an occasional visitor, or a local lobster boat pulling traps just offshore. Today, Halibut Point is a 67-acre state park. A visitor center tells the story of the sweeping history here; its adjacent World War II-era observation tower offers sweeping coastal views. What most visitors don't know is that the name, "Halibut Point," has nothing to do with fish.

"For sailing ships coming down from Maine," explains St. Germain, "once you got to this cape that sticks out into the ocean, you'd have to tack to go south toward Rockport or Gloucester Harbor."

"You'd have to haul in and reset your sails for the wind."

"Exactly," St. Germain continues. "So the call from the captain was to 'Haul about!,' and switch the sails around to get down here. And somehow, over time, that became 'Halibut.' Everything gets shortened up, right?"

Thankfully, the views here have stayed as full-length and as expansive as ever.

⤛◆⤜

Less than 5 miles south of Halibut Point and Pigeon Cove, Route 127 winds its way along the water to downtown Rockport. There are few harbor towns as picturesque as Rockport. Indeed, search for info on Rockport and you'll find multiple descriptions that contain some version of "It looks straight out of a painting." It should. It's been in enough of them. In fact, it's often been said that the town's most iconic landmark—the red fishing shack on Bradley Wharf—has ended up in more paintings and photos than, well, almost *anything*.

"It's fun to hear the tourists walk by Motif Number One. They'll say it's the most photographed, the most painted object in Massachusetts, in the United States, in the world!" howls Mark Kanegis. "Love to know how people know that. I'm thinking the Eiffel Tower and the Great Wall of China could be up there."

A native of Rockport, Mark Kanegis has lived there most of his life. He's an accomplished landscape photographer who loves Cape Ann, and has photographed it extensively over the years. His photos peek out from the walls of homes, coffeehouses, and other local businesses

MOTIF NO. 1. (MARK KANEGIS)

with the familiarity of an old friend. He is, in fact, a longtime friend of mine. We've met up on a drizzly spring morning at Hula Moon, a lively little family-run breakfast spot on the harbor in the heart of town. There's nothing remotely Hawaiian on the menu; lots of sharp Vermont cheddar in my omelet, though.

Mark's been chatting up a couple of older guys (older than Mark, not necessarily me). One, with a trim, white beard and a Bruins cap, says he's in here almost every day.

"It's kinda like being in your kitchen and hanging out with—well, that's the thing." He laughs loudly as he gestures around the room. "Unfortunately it's the same people every day!"

"Including you," I offer.

"Exactly!" he howls with laughter. "Including me!"

Mark and I stroll a block over to the harbor's center, and T-Wharf. Little activity in the chilly, gray mist. Motif No. 1's rich, red exterior stands out as the lone splash of color. I look around; it's rare not to see someone, anyone, taking a quick photo, or in summer, not to see at least a few people sitting at an easel painting the same scene. Does this famous little fishing shack really seem to pop up everywhere like a bad penny? Kind of.

"Funny story," Mark says, smiling as we both stare out at the water. "Guy comes into my old gallery on Bearskin Neck. Businessman, on vacation, and he buys one of my photos of Motif Number One. Perfect picture of New England to take home. He goes to China on business. He's in a restaurant, goes to the restroom—there's a picture of Motif Number One on the wall!"

America's (allegedly) most famous fishing shack began life as just a regular, anonymous fishing shack. Story goes that a local Rockport High School art teacher would annually assign his students to go out and paint something typical of Cape Ann. The simple, weathered red fishing shack covered with colorful lobster buoys proved to be an irresistible subject. So much so that the teacher, frustrated that students weren't looking for more interesting subjects to paint, threw up his hands one day and said, "Once again, nothing but motif number one!" The name stuck. Today, it's not even the original shack. The original was blown off its foundation in the famous Blizzard of 1978. An authentic replica replaced it.

We are about to get in out of a chilly drizzle when Mark, friendly with many of the fishermen and lobstermen here, spots a familiar face on a familiar boat at the dock. Captain Billy Lee, a sprightly seventy-something with playful eyes, a quick laugh, and white hair under his cap, fished commercially for thirty-seven years. Today he works in Rockport's harbor, maintaining moorings for other boat owners.

"You guys look like you could use a roof over your heads right about now," he yells over, seeing Mark. "Hop on!"

So we do, sidling in on either side of Lee under the *Ocean Reporter*'s small cockpit canopy. I ask Lee if he misses fishing.

"On a crappy day like this one? Ha!"

His radio belches some static; he reaches up and turns down the volume.

"I miss going up to the coffee shops in Gloucester in the morning when the wind was blowing and we weren't fishing and all the fishermen would get together over a cup and we'd all lie to each other about how we were doing."

"No need to lie now," Mark interjects. "Everyone knows everyone's doing lousy."

"No need to lie now 'cause there's no *fishermen*!" Lee roars with a laugh. "Look, there's still a lot of hardworking lobstermen out of Rockport, but there's only a few fishermen left, and they usually go scalloping or hooking for codfish in the winter. So I guess now we're gonna have to finally say this is officially a tourist town."

I joke that his work nowadays keeps him motoring around tourist attraction number one. "You guys ever been inside it?"

"Just filled with fishing gear, right?" says Mark.

"*Ground* floor, yeah," Lee says with a wide grin. "You ain't been *up*stairs."

With one hand on his wheel, leaning over to check his distance from the dock, he then deftly swings wide away, pulls on the visor of his cap, and returns his focus to the water. "C'mon, I'll show ya."

In less than five minutes, he makes a big, arcing half-circle around the end of the main wharf, sliding in toward Motif No. 1, cutting

CAPTAIN BILLY LEE AND MARK KANEGIS, ABOARD THE *OCEAN REPORTER.*

his engine, and in one smooth, expert motion, bringing his boat softly and snugly up against the dock at Bradley Wharf.

We hop out onto the dock, tie up, climb up a short ladder to the top of the wharf, and are an arm's length from the most famous side of the famous little shack. We follow Billy Lee, a man on a mission, as he walks quickly to the door and swings it open for us. Dark and dingy, fishing and boat equipment is every-where; ropes, buoys, nets, oars, outboard motors.

"By the way," Lee yells over his shoulder as he walks rapidly toward the stairway, "this space ain't free—guys pay the town for the storage space."

We follow him up the narrow and creaky wooden stairs.

When Mark and I reach the top, Billy is already standing a few feet inside the attic-like room.

"Welcome." He grins, spreading his arms wide as if to embrace it all.

There's a lot to embrace. None of it anything I'd expected. The room itself is small, maybe fifteen or twenty feet square, with three small dormer windows, one on each of the two sides, and one facing out the rear of the building. There's no empty space; it took some maneuvering just for the three of us to stand and move about a bit. The small room—walls, ceiling—is literally stuffed full with what looks like basic antiques and bric-a-brac. There does seem to be an undeniable nautical theme. Not the hanging disco ball, or the scuffed-up tenor sax next to it. But both share airspace with a fully rigged ship model, a crusty, yellowing sou'wester hat, and a genuine old wooden ship's wheel. Oh, and a nearly life-size pink plastic mermaid.

"No pictures of the mermaid, please," Lee says matter-of-factly.

"So, Billy," I say, after wiping some dust off the sax, looking for a date, "in addition to being the guy who takes care of all the moorings in the harbor, you're also the curator of the secret and unofficial Motif Number One Museum."

"Ha! Yes, that's true!"

Truthfully, Lee doesn't mind sharing this mostly secret haunt.

"My wife's been up here a few times with her girlfriends; they have coffee, look around."

Most of the visitors, though, are older, married guys who've been told to get rid of some old object that is dear to them but junk to anyone else. They can't bear to trash it, so they bring it to Billy Lee, who adds it to his collection.

"You love keeping this little place up," I say.

"I do, of course I do. But I'm seventy-three now, coming up on retirement, so in the next few years, I'm going to pass the torch to one of the younger guys."

When that happens, there'll be no official ceremony. All the people walking by and taking their selfies will still have no idea this crazy collection exists. All of which leaves me with a newfound fondness for what I have long regarded as just a clichéd and overexposed tourist landmark. Turns out, there is more than meets the eye to the iconic (if replica) fishing shack that countless artists and visitors have reverentially painted and photographed for decades. Make no mistake—the famous exterior that they paint and shoot *is* an artificial, overexposed, and clichéd tourist landmark. But the *inside* that they'll never see is actually a retired fishermen's secret man-cave. There's a wonderful lesson in there somewhere about not judging books by their covers. Or shacks by their shutters.

—⫷⫸—

Motif No. 1 aside, there is, in fact, a long history of great artists creating great work on Cape Ann. It's an enduring part of its identity, as ingrained now as the water, the fishing, and the granite itself. It's especially true in Gloucester.

THE CLAM BOX

(Ipswich, MA)

THE CLAM BOX, IPSWICH, MASSACHUSETTS. (MARK KANEGIS)

MA Route 133 on Cape Ann is sometimes referred to as the "Clam Highway."

Such is the love affair here with fried clams. After all, from the Cape's clam beds in and around Ipswich come some of the country's tastiest clams. Adding to the lore here, Woodman's in Essex has long claimed to be the birthplace of the fried clam in 1916. Today, Woodman's is one of the best places to get fried clams on Cape Ann.

Its Essex neighbor, Farnham's, is also really good. Only 5 miles away, in Ipswich, the Clam Box stakes its own claim to clam dominance. If the judges were also counting architectural creativity and originality, the Clam Box wins. Built in 1935, the building resembles a giant, shingled take-out box. Inside, there's an order window and a single dining room; in warmer weather, most people prefer to sit outside at a picnic table. And the clams? As good as I've ever had.

The late Chickie Aggelakis, the guiding force (and force of nature) of the modern Clam Box, swore the difference here was that (unlike most places) they change the fryer oil twice a day. Takes more time (they close for twenty minutes every afternoon), more money, but it was a point of pride for Aggelakis. "Woodman's may have invented the fried clam," she liked to say, "but I perfected it."

The customers who troop here from all over seem to think so. On a visit in 2021, I asked a guy who'd driven nearly 40 miles for lunch what he thought. "I've had fried clams all over Massachusetts," he said, brandishing a golden one still on his plastic fork. "This is the place I judge all other clam places by."

Clearly, the judges have reached a decision.

Continuing south on Route 127 along the water from Rockport harbor, past Whale Cove, Loblolly Cove, the twin lights of Thacher Island, and Good Harbor Beach, it's only a drive of 5 miles or so to Gloucester Harbor, where 127 empties out into Eastern Avenue, and the storied seaport opens up before you.

Less than halfway up the city side of the inner harbor, on a little hill on the right, is Fitz Henry Lane Park, named for the early- to mid-nineteenth-century seascape master painter, who was born in Gloucester in 1804. Sitting on a small perch of granite is a bronze likeness of Lane himself, body braced to the wind, sketchpad and brush in hand, leaning in resolutely to capture the scene of the sea and the harbor just below.

FISHERMAN'S MEMORIAL, GLOUCESTER.
(MARK KANEGIS)

Less than a mile just west, past the town landing and St. Peter's Park, stands the Fisherman's Memorial, and another bronze statue. It's the figure of a sailor, in full oilskin sou'wester, also leaning resolutely into the wind and sea, his hands forever gripping a ship's wheel, above the famous inscription in stone, *They that go down to the sea in ships* . . . Close by each other, each focused on the sea in their respective tasks, the two statues are also symbols of a closeness that is both unique and defining for Gloucester.

"Obviously, the Natives, then the fishermen, were here first," says Courtney Richardson, director of Gloucester's Rocky Neck Art Colony. "But since the nineteenth century artists were drawn to this area, and then this relationship between the two—the artists and the fishermen—they just learned to live and work together."

Rocky Neck, a small, narrow peninsula that juts out into Gloucester Harbor, is home to one of the oldest continuously operating art colonies in America. Its narrow streets, lined with small, colorful galleries and artist studios, weave alongside the harbor at every turn. Great artists have painted this very view—Edward Hopper, Winslow Homer, John Sloan, Fitz Henry Lane, Emil Gruppe—entranced a century ago by the same things that hold my gaze on this sunny spring afternoon: the blue-green water in the harbor, the weathered wooden docks, the reflected light on the fishing boats tied up to them.

"By now, after all these years, we coexist like an old couple," says Mark Kanegis, laughing when he speaks about what he describes as the "roughly fifty-fifty" mix between the artists and the remaining fishermen and lobstermen here. "We get along well. But I think there are days when the artists who're cooped up in the galleries wish they were on the boats, and there are certainly days when the waves are big and the fishermen wish they were inside a cozy gallery."

From the fishing side, Joe Sanfilippo's family has been part of that unique mix here for generations.

"More than four hundred years of fishing here. And the Natives, the painters, the artists, it's all really molded it into something special. But in the end, we're a fishing town. Still. That's what we are."

A slim, taut, late-forties guy with a shaved head and a goatee, Sanfilippo moves with a quick and intense energy. The youngest of five brothers, he describes fishing and his family in Gloucester as "generational." He started fishing on an older brother's boat when he was eleven.

"Everyone fished—Dad, all of Dad's brothers, all of Mom's brothers, all of my brothers, and pretty much all of my nieces and nephews—we've all fished at one point or another."

Alas, few are still fishing. In Gloucester today, "R&R" does not mean "Rest & Relaxation." It means "Rules & Regs." Since the late 1970s, federal and state efforts have tried to stem the dramatic decline in Northeast fish stocks, particularly cod. Entire offshore fishing grounds, like the famed Georges Bank or Stellwagen Bank, can be suddenly closed entirely, with little notice. Catch and species limits are rigidly enforced and checked at sea. Fines can be swift and significant. Has it all helped? Tough to say. The efforts can be, and are, endlessly debated. Maybe, as in Newfoundland, where the cod simply disappeared, it's all too late, anyway. What's clear is that, for the most part, fishermen feel the regs have been wielded like blunt instruments that help little and hammer indiscriminately. It's left fishermen here (or those that are left) feeling frustrated, dazed, battered, and helpless.

Years back, I recall talking to a fisherman who was curiously offloading equipment and unused ice chests at dawn, when he should have been on-loading them.

"Nothing doing today," he said, tossing some extra line onto the dock. "Rolling closure just announced for Jeffreys Ledge."

He was a day fisherman, heading out daily for twelve hours, going after haddock, cod, yellowtail flounder, and whatever else was open and available. The sudden closure forced him to send his two-man crew home.

"Sucks, but nothin' new," he said, slowly taking off his heavy rubber gloves. "Ain't gonna feed my family this way."

Joe Sanfilippo knew that fisherman. He relates.

"I bought my own boat when I was twenty-eight. Bought an eighty-foot dragger, called it *The Lucky.*" He looks across at the quiet warehouse on the opposite dock, laughs quietly to himself. "*The Lucky.*"

After years of commercial fishing, years of mounting frustration, Sanfilippo got to the same place so many others here got to. He had to give it up.

"The amount of stress it takes now just to leave the dock, it's so tough. And the regs . . ." He looks down at the water, shakes his head. "It's almost impossible for anyone new to get into the game anymore."

Joe Sanfilippo, Gloucester Harbor, Massachusetts. (Bob Oliver)

"How many fishermen do you know personally who've been put out of work?" I ask.

"Over the last twenty years or so? Hundreds. Easily. These are people who put twenty, thirty years into a career and had to change. It's devastating."

⤙⤙⟡⤚⤚

In finding a life after fishing, Sanfilippo was more fortunate than some. He's been able to stay on the water. He's captain and engineer on the *Beauport*, a large Gloucester Harbor cruise boat. On a damp and overcast morning, we stand just outside the *Beauport*'s bridge, against the ship's rail, surveying the sweep of the inner harbor below us. It's quiet; there's little activity, lots of unused dock space. Several older, former fishing-related buildings are in various stages of falling apart. More than a century ago, at the height of Gloucester's fishing prosperity, the inner harbor looked like a forest of masts; it was said a person could walk around the horseshoe harbor, stepping from fishing boat to fishing boat, never getting a foot wet. Now, it's as if the forest has been clear-cut.

"How many working boats would you say are in the harbor now?" I ask.

"Probably about sixty working boats," he says after a pause. "Which is a fraction of what it once was. And quite a few of them are day boats. Very few boats, maybe eight, go out offshore for a week. Which is really, really sad."

But Sanfilippo does more than just lament the sad state of fishing here. He started Extreme Gloucester Fishing, which he describes as a "sustainable fisheries learning center." On the second floor of a building on the Gloucester waterfront, he teaches and provides hands-on learning in a classroom setting. It's like night school for fishermen: marine safety, vessel handling, fishing methods and terminology, net repair, policies and regulations.

"Between my dad's boat and my brother's first boat, I would say at least three hundred people were trained to fish. That's gone. That generational pipeline is gone. So the mission is to create new fishermen, 'cause once you lose entirely what we have here, it's all gone. The knowledge will never return; you won't get it back."

It's almost mid-morning now; Sanfilippo has a workday to get started on. I hesitate to ask him, but I do.

"Do you miss fishing?"

He grips the ship's rail and looks out in the distance, past Ten Pound Island Light at the harbor's mouth. "Absolutely. Every minute of every day. As hard as it was, as much time as it took away from my family . . ."

There's a sudden loud whine of an electric sander. Sanfilippo turns and looks intently at the dry dock below us, where a stern-trawler's hull is being worked on.

"I can't explain the feeling," he says quietly, looking back out at the water, tapping the railing a few times with his open hand. "You ask most fishermen, they'll say the same thing: It's something that lives inside of you."

-⫷⬦⫸-

A year or so after spending that morning with Joe Sanfilippo, his words came to mind on another stop in Gloucester. I was drawn to an exhibit at the city's wonderful Cape Ann Museum: *The Legacy of the Family-Owned Fishing Vessel*. Part celebration, part elegy, the exhibit stood as a stark reminder that what was once commonplace in Gloucester—a family-owned fishing boat—had become as rare as bountiful catches.

In the seaport's golden age, the harbor brimmed with five hundred or so fishing vessels, most of them family-owned. Today, only about seventy-five

MICHAEL FRONTIERO REPAIRING FISHING NET WITH SON, PAUL (1938). (PHOTO COURTESY OF PAUL FRONTIERO)

family-owned boats remain. The exhibit focused on the most personal part of Gloucester's long and rich maritime history—that it was created mostly by brave and hardworking individuals, and their equally dedicated families. They were Italian, Portuguese, West Indian, Canadian. Mostly nineteenth-century immigrants, they worked on boats, many eventually managed to own one, and if they were lucky, they worked them tirelessly for decades, often handing off ownership to one of their children or another relative.

Over time, the boat might be modernized or replaced, but the family's fishing connection endured, through a boat that was beloved, prized, and valued like family itself.

"Their boat protected them out there, and that's why they took such care of them," says Nina Goodick, who grew up and still lives in Gloucester., where she is the rare person who combines both the artistic and fishing traditions here. Goodick is a professional potter, a member of the Rocky Neck Art Colony, and helped to create the exhibit. She's also the fifth generation of a Gloucester fishing family.

"My dad was always on the boat. If I wanted to find him, I'd go down to the wharf. If he wasn't fishing, he was down there taking care of the engine. They had to be mechanics as well as fishermen. They took care of the boats because the boat took care of them."

Goodick and I are standing in a mostly empty gallery room at the museum on an early September morning. The exhibit is unique in that it was not curated by museum staff, but rather as a community effort. Local families lent significant mementos—photographs, pieces of equipment, and especially homemade boat models and paintings of their boats.

"Growing up, my family and all my friends who were fishing families would always have a painting of their fishing vessel on the wall. We weren't a family of means by any measure," says Goodick. "We didn't have art, but we always had a painting of our boat. And it was because she sustained us, she took care of us. And we were very proud of her."

The pride in the room is evident. Black-and-white photos of young fishermen beaming from the bows of their boats, decks busy with their small crew, freshly hauled nets bristling with big catches of cod.

"A lot of these men had dropped out of school, learning fishing at such a young age—seventh grade, they're out of school—they'd been taught by their fathers how to fish, and then they're learning the fishing trade and going on and getting their own boats," explains Goodick, as we stop at a painting. She smiles as she points at it.

FISHING TRAWLER, GLOUCESTER, MASSACHUSETTS. (MARK KANEGIS)

"Like my uncle Paul in that painting, mending a net. Suddenly they're running their own business. It was their boat. They loved their boats and no detail was too small to ignore. It was a great sense of pride for them."

Goodick and I have a laugh next to an old and weathered brass ship's bell. She knows it well.

"Yeah, this is my doorbell," she smiles, shaking her head.

"This former ship's bell?"

"It was on the *Linda B.*, which was my grandfather's and my dad's boat."

"So your house has no doorbell right now."

"No." She laughs. "Not until this comes back!"

Goodick also points out an oddity in the exhibit—the only representation of a family-owned fishing vessel that is still operative, still in the water, still fishing. It's a model of her uncle Tom Testaverde's boat, *Midnight Sun*. It's a sleek, newer trawler, gleaming white deck over a dark blue hull.

"She's still active, every season she's allowed to go out, whatever their fishing days' allotted time is, she's active," she says proudly.

THE *MARIA AND AL*.

Some of the fishing boat models are extraordinary in their craftsmanship and detail. Many, if not most, were made by their owners, fishermen who had lovingly and painstakingly created likenesses of their beloved boats. Like the *Maria and Al*.

"When he first started making models, he was just a deckhand on a boat," explains Al Millefoglie, son of Alphonse Millefoglie, who would go on to captain his own boat. Al and his sister, Maria, have stopped by the exhibit.

"Not everyone gets a boat named after them," I say, as the three of us stand by the boat model, admiring its craftsmanship. Sadly, their dad was moved to make the model when the real boat sank following an electrical fire.

"He'd been ready to retire in like, another five years," Al says. "I think he just needed to see his boat again."

I ask Al and Maria if they can show me where their dad's boat used to dock. We head down to Gloucester Harbor and stand at the end of the dock where the boat tied up.

"So this is a pretty familiar view for you both, huh?" I say.

"Oh, yeah," nods Al, with a smile of recollection. "Especially when they came in from fishing after seven days. Usually my mom, our grandmother, everybody would be waiting at the dock to give 'em a hug and a kiss after being out for so long."

As we stand in the breezy but delightful warmth of the late-day sun, Maria makes a final point about the lives that their father and all these fishermen—and their families—had led.

"Growing up, Al and I didn't have the gift of seeing our father much. He was at sea, and it was the women who had to manage the household, pay the bills, discipline the kids."

Looking down, then over at the boats, her brother nods quietly.

"So it was a difficult life, it wasn't a romantic life," she adds. "It was really, really difficult. But there's a special breed of men that came here from Sicily, the Azores, all over. They came with nothing, came with a dream, and they made a life at sea."

"Does that still happen here?" I ask.

"Yes. People are still fishing today, there's still wonderful bravery and courage going on today. But that day of our father's, what it was like here then, that part's gone. Those men are gone. But they taught us something, and they left us an amazing legacy."

It's late afternoon. We say our good-byes. Al still lives nearby; Maria has to drive back up to her home in southern Maine. The harbor is quiet. The sun, in the west now, has lit up the water. On the opposite side of the harbor, a puff of black exhaust smoke catches my eye, then the telltale hum of a boat engine revving up. A moment later, a blue-and-white trawler clears its dock, foaming wake gathering behind it as it slowly picks up speed. I squint to read the nameplate on the boat's pilothouse side. My eyes widen: *Midnight Sun.* Not the model, the real boat, with Captain Tom Testaverde at the wheel, I assume. I fold my arms, smiling at this unexpected sight. There's life here yet.

The *Midnight Sun* passes out of view, trailing a faint spume of exhaust. A slight turn to starboard, and she'd quickly be passing Ten Pound Island Light, making for open sea. There was fishing to do.

GLOUCESTER HARBOR. (MARK KANEGIS)

—≪≪◆≫≫—

CHAPTER 4

Into New Hampshire,
onto the Coast (Don't Blink)

Old Route 1. Never seems to change, never gets far from the Atlantic. Sure, Interstate 95 is faster and covers the same basic north–south route along the East Coast of the United States. But it's not local, and that's the whole reason to be on Route 1: It's more local.

Route 1 extends 2,390 miles from Fort Kent, Maine, to Key West, Florida. In Florida, and again in the Northeast, it tightly hugs the coastline. (In its early decades, it was called the "Atlantic Highway.") Coming off of Cape Ann and heading north, the just-under-thirty-minute drive from Ipswich, Massachusetts, over the border to Seabrook, New Hampshire, is about 25 miles. That's about 7 miles more than the entire coastline of New Hampshire itself. Don't blink. At 18.57 miles, it's the shortest seacoast of any state. But not without note.

"Don't laugh—there are real waves in New Hampshire!"

Dave Cropper isn't having any of my smirk and raised eyebrows.

"A lot of people will show up here when the waves are good, when there are two hundred people surfing, and they're like, whoa!"

"You mean, they're like, wait—this is *New Hampshire*?"

"Exactly. They're surprised. This is a surprising coastline."

On a trip in the spring of 2018, I wanted to find some folks who really loved the state's small coastline, made their life on it, and didn't make jokes about it. Dave Cropper was one of them.

"For a small coastline, there are some great point breaks that'll hold big waves, and in the summer when the waves are small, we have great sand-bottom beaches for beginners."

"But it's *New Hampshire*, Dave, right?" I smiled. "Not Hawaii."

"Okay, we're gonna get you out there, wise guy!"

He almost did, too.

Cropper opened his surf shop, Cinnamon Rainbows Surf Co., in 1983. It's right on the beach. It may not be Malibu, but Cropper, a fifty-something blond guy with a friendly laugh and a boyish manner, looks like a California surfer right out of central casting. He loves the area, loves the water, and especially his devoted surfer friends here. And he loves sharing it.

"Surfing with Smiles" began a bit by chance. A kid with special needs wondered if he could take a surfing lesson. Cropper and another instructor found a way. Then they found a way for some others. Word got out, more requests, so other surfing instructors volunteered to help. Now, on a few dates every summer, anyone who wants to get out on a surfboard gets out on a surfboard. Period. Even if they're generally in a wheelchair.

DAVE CROPPER, NORTH HAMPTON, NEW HAMPSHIRE.

"Some kids, they get up on the board and they yell and they're blown away—they can't believe what they're doing," says Cropper, laughing. "For some kids, it's just getting in the water, just sitting or laying back quietly on a surfboard while we hold it, feeling the swell under them. They look up at the sky, they look at the water, they smile. It's just so different for them. It's amazing to see."

Cropper takes a big breath. "It's the highlight of my summer. Every year."

—◄◄◆►►—

Route 1A branches off of Route 1 at Hampton, and runs right alongside the water for the entire short drive up the New Hampshire coast. Surprising waves aside, it's not a pretty coastline. The beaches are small and stubbly, mostly bordered by an ever-present concrete seawall on one side, and too much development on the other. And while some pockets along the way, like the town of Rye, are affluent with multimillion-dollar beach homes, other spots, like Hampton Beach, are honky-tonk shitholes that are less geared to the ocean than to bars, bikers, and buck-a-beer nights. Hey, takes a village.

Ironically, some of the prettiest views on the New Hampshire seacoast are offshore. The Isles of Shoals are comprised of nine small islands 6 miles off the coast. They're isolated out in the far western reach of the Gulf of Maine; the state boundary between Maine and New Hampshire actually runs through half of the islands. Two of them—Smuttynose and Appledore—sound like characters out of *Harry Potter*. There's long and colorful history out here, from early explorers like John Smith, and later on, pirates, famous painters, and writers, even a gruesome double murder in 1837. Around 1700, the residents of Appledore all moved over to Star Island to escape taxes levied by Massachusetts (whose borders at that time included Maine). Clearly, New Hampshire's residents have never been big on taxes. On Star Island today, you can stay overnight at a rustic hotel with a big porch and watch amazing sunsets over the ocean, free of charge. (The view, not the room—which will include state taxes.)

Back on land and the winding, asphalt sea serpent that is 1A, I spent a brilliantly sunny late spring morning in Rye, where I was headed to the beach. It was dead-low tide, but that was the plan. I was running down a story that seemed like something out of a sci-fi movie, but also seemed not to get the larger play it warranted. Gabby Bradt, a marine biologist with both the University of New Hampshire and New Hampshire Sea Grant, couldn't agree more.

"They're an invasive species, they're voracious, they basically eat everything in sight, their favorite food is any kind of shellfish, and they are decimating whole populations on the East Coast."

"Other than that, Gabby," I laugh, "what don't we like about green crabs?"

"They're also hurting us in the pocketbook—their populations have exploded, so if you're a commercial shell fisherman, this is big trouble out there."

Odds are, you haven't heard of—much less considered—the undersea life of the lowly green crab. Gabby Bradt considers little else these days. Green crabs, known officially as *Carcinus maenas*, have earned the unofficial name "Most Malicious Mollusk." They've been around the East Coast of the United States since the late 1800s, likely having hitched a ride on a merchant vessel from Europe. Marine biologists consider them one of the single most invasive species in the entire marine environment. They have few predators, and routinely out-compete other local species for both food and habitat. Needless to say, they are lousy neighbors and aren't making any new friends. They've now spread to the West Coast as well, where there is mounting fear they may seriously damage Alaska's multibillion-dollar seafood industry.

"So the green crab problem is bad and it's gotten worse, yes?"

"Yes, it's gotten much worse," Gabby says, as she bends over to push aside a large rock. "It has invaded all the way up to Prince Edward Island."

For half an hour, she and I have been scouring a rocky Rye beach at low tide; we each have a big orange bucket, but they're empty.

"Here's one!" She holds up a pentagon-shaped greenish crab-looking thing with claws, barely two inches wide.

"That's not very impressive," I observe. "Definitely not scary-looking."

"I know, right?" she says, as she drops it with a thump into the bucket. "You wouldn't think they were wreaking havoc up and down the coast. But they eat anything in sight."

GABBY BRADT WITH GREEN CRAB, RYE, NEW HAMPSHIRE. (UNIVERSITY OF NEW HAMPSHIRE)

Clearly. According to Bradt, a midsize green crab, only two to three inches across, can eat up to fifty mussels a day. But Bradt is also one of a small group of experts who've not only been tracking the green crab invasion, but have come up with a possible solution: If you can't beat 'em—eat 'em.

"In Venice, Italy, they've turned it into a lucrative, fancy food," says Bradt. "It's not easy, 'cause you have to get them at the right time molting-wise, so you get the soft shell, but they taste good, and we're getting more and more interest."

"Are chefs getting on board?"

"Yes, we've had more and more tell us that if we can get them more, they can sell them."

"That's where the fishermen come in, right? This would create a financial incentive for them to get at these green crabs that are hurting them, anyway."

"Yes," she says, "but we must develop and create the markets for them. We're working on it!"

It's close to noon. The sun is higher now on the beach, and it's warmed up. People are walking the beach, some wading along the shoreline; spring is in the air. Gabby Bradt and I make our way back up to her truck. She lets the lift gate down and I help her put her orange buckets on the truck bed.

"You've become like the green crab lady," I say, laughing.

"I think so, yeah," she says, shaking her head.

The real comic irony, which she shares only now as we're leaving, is that she loathes crabs—all crabs.

"I'd even call it a phobia," she says quietly, lest anyone should overhear.

"But look what you do for work! What a great way to conquer it!"

"I have conquered it," she says matter-of-factly, kicking off one of her green rubber boots. "I get hung up on things as a scientist, and the green crab thing has been a huge puzzle! It's really hurting fishermen, and I really wanted to try and help solve it."

—‹‹‹◆›››—

On into Portsmouth, a great, old port city. (Plus it sits on a river whose name—Piscataqua—is just plain fun to say out loud.) Being nearby was an opportunity to meet up and reconnect with another woman doing some great things in the area. A year earlier, in south-central New Hampshire, I had made the acquaintance of JerriAnne Boggis. She'd asked me in an earlier phone call if I knew anything about Harriet E. Wilson. I told her I didn't.

"You should know about her," Boggis said.

She was right. Everyone should know more about Harriet E. Wilson. In 1859, she became the first published Black novelist in North America. Nothing about her life could have predicted this pioneering achievement. Her parents, unable to care for her or feed an extra mouth, had left her as a young girl on the doorstep of a white family in Milford, New Hampshire. A free Black, she nonetheless became an indentured servant. She was also bright, brave, became highly literate, and was determined to tell her story.

"Everything she did was against the odds," says JerriAnne Boggis. "She wrote a book, and she was able to publish a book. Nobody thought she was intelligent enough to write and publish a book. Against the odds she became an entrepreneur, went out and found ways to sell her book, all by herself."

In her own life, JerriAnne Boggis has also been brave and bucked the odds. Born in Jamaica, she came to the United States when she was seventeen, settled in New England, earned an undergraduate degree in computer science, a master's degree in creative writing, and raised two sons. But it wasn't easy.

"I often felt like the only Black person in the whole state," recalls Boggis.

Black people comprise less than 2 percent of New Hampshire's population.

In 2002, living in Milford, New Hampshire, she was introduced to the story of one of the small town's most extraordinary, if little-known, native daughters, Harriet E. Wilson.

"It changed everything," says Boggis.

Inspired, Boggis began extensively researching Wilson's life. She also became determined to share Wilson's story and legacy.

"Because of Wilson, I began to identify more strongly and personally with my predominantly white town, because now I had a connection with its history, too," says Boggis. "And I wanted others like me to be able to feel that way, because it's often so hard in a place like New Hampshire."

Boggis led an effort that, in 2006, succeeded in creating a permanent memorial in Milford to its former resident, Harriet E. Wilson. A decade later, on a chilly, misty October morning, I stood with Boggis on the leaf-strewn but still-green grass of a small park by the meandering Souhegan River. On the statue's marble base, the chiseled inscription reads:

HARRIET E. WILSON
AUTHOR
1825-1900

HARRIET E. WILSON STATUE, MILFORD, NEW HAMPSHIRE.

Boggis and I stare up at Wilson's impressive, deep bronze face and strong features, which show a faint smile and an expression of purpose and pride. With one arm she holds her book, while the other sweeps back protectively around her young son, George, who seems to peek uncertainly from behind his mother's long skirt.

"We really wanted the town to acknowledge this history, to bring her to life in the town that she lived in," says Boggis, looking straight ahead, never breaking her gaze at the statue. "She is in a public space and that's what we wanted. This was her town, too."

"Safe to say," I ask, "that she's been more embraced in Milford today than when she lived here?"

"No question," nods Boggis. "But it's not just a Milford story, not just a New Hampshire story, or even a Black history story. It's an *American* story. And when we fully embrace the richness of our culture, the richness of our stories, we can truly look honestly at ourselves. Otherwise we can never repair what was damaged."

JERRIANNE BOGGIS. (BOB OLIVER)

"Is this what repair looks like?"

"It's a pretty good start," she says.

Reconnecting with Boggis in Portsmouth, we meet up at the visitor center and offices of the Black Heritage Trail of New Hampshire, which she helped to create, and where she's executive director.

It's a warm, sunny morning when we set out to walk the old streets of the city near the harbor. In three blocks, we are on the edge of Strawbery Banke, an outdoor history museum which comprises the oldest buildings in Portsmouth and is the state's oldest neighborhood, settled by Europeans. On Court Street, we stop on a cobblestone sidewalk in front of a restored, gray wooden, three-story colonial building. The William Pitt Tavern, built in 1766, is home to a hidden history that's as grim as it is surprising.

"You'd see an ad back then," says Boggis. "Maybe a handbill handed out in the square, around the wharfs. It would say, 'Come to Pitt's

Tavern Saturday, where we'll be selling cotton or cloth,' and then at the end, 'and two young boys.'"

"A slave auction."

"Yes, a slave auction."

"Of all the stops on the Black Heritage Trail here," I wonder, "do you find this is the one that surprises most people? Not just slavery here, in New Hampshire, but slave *auctions*, too."

"Absolutely. People are shocked to find out we had enslavement, and then, more shock—that we actually had auctions, just like in the South."

Portsmouth also figured in one of early America's most famous searches for a runaway slave. The slave was the property of two of history's most famous Americans: George and Martha Washington. Ona Judge had risen in the Washington household to become Martha's personal maid. But on a trip with the Washingtons to Philadelphia in 1796, Judge was deeply struck by the free Black community there. Only twenty-two, she fled, and was able to seek passage on a ship bound for Portsmouth, New Hampshire.

The Washingtons mounted an aggressive search for their escaped slave, which included sending an aide to the home of then New Hampshire governor, John Langdon. But Judge avoided detection and capture, and lived out her life—cautiously and discreetly—only 5 miles from Portsmouth.

"Never caught," I say to Boggis, as we stand in front of the wide, white Langdon mansion on Portsmouth's Pleasant Street. "But never truly freed, either."

"No, never caught, never freed," she nods. "But it's a great story of the deep, human *desire* for freedom, isn't it? Even living in such luxury—in the president's house, no less—as an enslaved person, it was much more important to her to try and find freedom."

Boggis and I wend our way slowly back to her office. We talk about the nature of history. I thank her for introducing me, over the course of a year, to the stories of two extraordinary women.

"Triumphant stories, too, even though we might not look at them and think that," smiles Boggis. "They were trying to make their own way, no matter what was put in front of them. Isn't that the hero's story that we all look up to? Isn't that the *American* story?"

GILLEY'S DINER

(Portsmouth, NH)

GILLEY'S DINER, PORTSMOUTH, NEW HAMPSHIRE.

Diners originated with the advent of 24/7 shiftwork at factories. Some of the earliest ones were also, essentially, the first food trucks—wagons hauled by horses to a site where workers could easily grab something simple and cheap when nothing else was open. Gilley's Diner harkens back to that long-ago experience. In 1912, "PM Lunch" began as just such a horse-pulled wagon, becoming a popular, daily fixture in Portsmouth's Market Square. (One of its first employees was a kid named Ralph Gilley, who, over nearly seventy years, would become as beloved a local fixture as the diner itself.) Even after the wagon gave way to a Worcester dining car in 1940, it still was hauled to its site—by truck—every morning. Only in 1974 was it permanently installed at its Fleet Street location, tucked in tightly against a city parking garage. The menu is limited but legendary: dogs, burgers, chili, fries. (You want a salad, go to the crunchy spot down the street.) Hell, even the fries were a new innovation by owner Steve Kennedy, who's run things with his wife, Gina, since 1993.

"We never had french fries, even though it's a burger joint," says Kennedy. "People told me, 'Gilley wouldn't be happy.' I said, Hey, I wanna do what's gonna keep us in business for another eighty years!"

Not sure he needs to worry. On my lunchtime visit on a sunny April day in 2021, a small line snaked out the door; others were devouring their hot dogs outside in the spring warmth. It had died down a bit by the time I went inside and ordered two dogs. Quieter now, I was able to park on a stool inside the small front dining area, where I devoured them with as much relish as they were covered with. Plus, I was able to compliment the chef—Kennedy himself on this day—who stood just a few feet away on the other side of the counter.

"Every town needs a place like this," he says, by way of acknowledgment. "It's one of those places that Americana is made of, and it's stood the test of time. I get to see grandfathers sitting right where you are, telling their grandchild about *his* first time in here. How great is that?"

From Portsmouth and the seacoast, it's a short detour inland to what is sometimes called New Hampshire's "hidden coast": Great Bay. Hard to imagine much of anything being hidden in southern New Hampshire, which itself is often jokingly referred to as "northern Massachusetts." Most of New Hampshire's population is located here, among its four most populous counties. Great Bay lies in two of those counties—Rockingham and Strafford—and touches mostly on the towns of Newington and Dover. It's close to Durham, home of the University of New Hampshire, and it's about 15 miles west of the seacoast city of Portsmouth.

This geography is significant. There are few major American marine estuaries that are as recessed and as far inland from the ocean as Great Bay. Encompassing almost 25,000 acres of tidal waters, it's one of the largest marine estuaries on the East Coast. Veering away from the ocean, off of 1A and onto 1 North, you're soon skirting the approach to Portsmouth. You're also skirting a marine marvel, passing through what is a thickly settled area, heavily developed for both residential and commercial use. Every day, thousands of commuters on major state roads and interstate drive by and even over the edges of the bay. They see water, to be sure; seven different rivers flow into it. But you're still on the edges. The undeveloped, watery expanse that is Great Bay is still lurking just out of view, hiding in plain sight.

"It's incredibly unique. You would never think you'd find this just fifteen miles from a city like Portsmouth," says Corey Riley. "It's a hidden gem."

"In an area that seems too busy and built up to hide anything!" I laugh.

"I'll tell you how hidden," Riley smiles, her hands held up for emphasis. "I grew up twenty minutes south of here, and I didn't even know the bay *existed* until I was an adult!"

Today, Riley is manager of the Great Bay National Estuarine Research Reserve, which works with the state's Department of Fish and Game in preserving, protecting, and managing the bay. It's a picture-perfect, sunny, warm early October afternoon when I finally have the opportunity to see the heart of the bay close up, away from the roads, noise, and people.

Riley and I meet up at one of the few public access points along the bay. She's nice enough to bring along two kayaks, and we carry them down to a small, wooden dock, just yards away from the University of New Hampshire's Jackson Estuarine Laboratory.

The first thing I notice is the pronounced movement of the water, like a river, which surprises me. Even more than 15 miles away, the ocean's effect is immediately evident.

"The tides can be extreme here," says Riley. "It's actually one of the most extreme tides on the East Coast, after the Bay of Fundy."

Only yards away, a pair of egrets has taken flight, water dropping and trailing from long legs as they rise and head east, toward the coast. Part of the Atlantic Flyway, nearly sixty separate species of waterfowl, shorebirds, and wading birds make the estuary home for at least part of the year. Most of the waterfowl that winter in the state's coastal area are found in Great Bay.

But birds are only part of the rich and diverse plant and animal life here.

"Over half the bay is just mud," points out Riley. "And that's where a lot of clams and razor clams thrive and the shorebirds come to feed. There are huge eelgrass beds which are an incredibly valuable habitat for all kinds of fish."

In short order, we're paddling out into the bay, at one of its widest points. One of my favorite things about being in a kayak is being low on the water, and small and light enough to drift easily with a current. On a day like this—seemingly alone on a saltwater expanse, barely above the water's surface, an immense, cloudless blue canopy stretching overhead—you feel small, speck-like, humbled. We both sit for a bit, not paddling, just taking in that sense of hugeness, beauty, and quiet.

GREAT BAY, NEW HAMPSHIRE. (BOB OLIVER)

"I know it's a weekday afternoon," I say. "Still, I can't get over that we have not had any company out here. Not a single boat. No one."

"True. All to ourselves—that's the hidden gem!" Riley laughs. "But it's also by design. There's not as many access points on Great Bay as there are on other waterways. There was a big push in the 1990s and early 2000s to protect the land surrounding the bay. That's why it's quiet and unspoiled. You have that buffer. There aren't any restaurants, not even much boat traffic."

"In other words, Corey, it could have ended up much different here."

"Oh, God, for sure. Much different."

We begin our paddle back. We lift ourselves out, onto the dock, and pull the kayaks up. I take a last long look out at the water.

"For all the times I've driven through the area, I cannot believe this is the first time I've gotten out onto the bay," I say.

"I hear that a lot." Riley laughs. "But it's good. That's why we really encourage people to get out and enjoy Great Bay. The only way you're going to fall in love with it and make sure you want to protect it is if you get to know it."

Heading up from the water, I turn back to look. The sun is lower now, just above the tree line way out on the other side. The water still looks a deep, cobalt blue under the same immense blue sky. A loon breaks the surface near the dock. No other activity in my entire view. Just water, trees, sky, stillness. Just 15 miles from a city. And the northern end of America's shortest seacoast.

CHAPTER 5

Heading Downeast, to Maine
(North, to Flatlanders)

Just past Portsmouth and the Piscataqua River lies Kittery, the first dot on the map in Maine. There are two ways to get through Maine's most southern corner: fast, and faster. I say this as someone who loves Maine deeply. It's a very big state with so much that is impressive and breathtaking, unique and memorable. Little of which is to be found in its first 35 miles.

Not that the ocean isn't pretty. But to see it, you'll need to bypass Interstate 95 / Maine Turnpike and opt instead for the slower Route 1. Passing through Kittery, York, and Ogunquit, it can be tough to get a good look at the water past the T-shirt shops, tourist traps, and the fifth or sixth "Captain Billy's deep-sea-fishing-fried clams-whale-watching-and-whatnot," all of which you'll pass repeatedly in one form or another between Kittery and Kennebunk.

Ten miles further north, Maine gets more interesting. It's not the Maine of tall, endless pine trees; that's inland and more than 300 miles further north. It's not yet the working, authentic fishing villages and small harbors with docks piled high with lobster traps. Those are further northeast along the coast, or, as they say in a classic New England-ism, "Downeast."

Just past Kennebunk, you're in Biddeford. Still very much in southern Maine, but for now, you've left the tourist trail behind. After all, who's interested in a battered, old mill town that watched its jobs and prosperity pick up and leave it like some poor stiff at a bar who's been stuck with the check at closing time? Me. I love Biddeford. It's the whole New England story, right there on the Saco River.

Like all the other once-mighty mill towns around New England, Biddeford's identity was shaped by a powerful river. The Saco is Maine's fourth-largest river, running over 130 miles through northern New Hampshire down into southern Maine before reaching the coast and emptying into Saco Bay. The river also forms the boundary between Biddeford and its sister city, Saco, on the northern side. They are different places, distinguished by geography. The native Abenaki fished and hunted along the Saco here a thousand years before the Pilgrims landed. The first European settler arrived in 1616. The powerful river seemed to beckon all those who beheld it. Eventually, the rapids and the falls on the Biddeford side brought the mills, legions of labor drawn from all over the world, and by the nineteenth century, made the city a textile industry powerhouse. The mill owners built their fortunes in Biddeford; they built their mansions across the river in Saco.

"People forget how big the Pepperell Mills here used to be," says Alan Casavant. "I had relatives, for example, in World War Two, they were working for Pepperell in the Philippines when the Japanese took over, so it was a worldwide operation."

By the time Casavant was a teenager here, the worldwide operation had shrunk back to Biddeford. Then it shrunk further to nothing at all.

"When I was a little kid, Biddeford was the focal point of York County. Main Street was booming, there were shops, stores, and people. It was a great place to grow up. Then, by the 1980s, I saw the change happen."

Casavant, a soft-spoken and genial fifty-something guy with a bushy beard and glasses looks like a college professor. He was, in fact, a longtime high school teacher who, when we first met up in his city hall office in 2019, was entering his fourth term as Biddeford's popular mayor. Recalling the city's darker days, he leans back in his chair and looks pensively out the window, where the top floor of the neighboring nineteenth-century brick mill building seems close enough to touch.

"It wasn't pretty, that period, that's for sure. First, the malls opened up just out of town, and that just pulled people away. Then the recession hit, and the mills that were left here just up and left for cheaper labor in the South and overseas. Where once there were easily ten thousand employees and people walking the streets, now there were three or four hundred. The whole dynamic in the city changed entirely."

Then there was the debacle of the incinerator that was approved and installed at great cost in the late 1980s. Billed as a jobs and revenue generator for the city, it instead became a smoke-belching albatross, an environmental hazard and an embarrassing mistake. Eventually it was closed down, but there it stood, its giant steel stack a rusting, hulking symbol of a city's sad demise.

"That had to be a painful period."

"I'll tell you truthfully," says Casavant, rolling a pencil between his fingers. "It almost felt like Biddeford had been scorned. Just, you know, by everyone and everything. Yeah, it was pretty tough."

But here's the remarkable thing about many of New England's former mill towns: They turn out to be as enduring and resilient as the rivers that run through them.

While the companies that built mills and made fortunes may pack up and leave, the towns they made millions in don't have that option. The mill buildings themselves are built like fortresses, and cost additional fortunes to raze and remove. So they simply stand where they are, mostly abandoned, aging proudly in place through the economic downturns and the deepening miseries of unemployment, crime, and drugs all around them. In cities and mill towns all over New England, these buildings often sit mute for decades, immense but irrelevant, silent testaments to better days gone by.

But the rivers outside them keep flowing, and times, and economies, keep changing. The same mill buildings that were too expensive to tear down become too irresistible to ignore for new industries and creative developers. It happened in Manchester, New Hampshire, and in Lawrence, Lowell, and Haverhill, Massachusetts. And it happened in Biddeford.

In 2012, the incinerator tower was demolished. A deep-pocketed Maine developer with vision and money stepped in to buy up the mill properties. Weathering the Great Recession, the massive redevelopment project inched forward, attracting residential and commercial tenants, from breweries to backpack makers, along with a range of artists and craftspeople. Locals have been cheered not just by the economic boost itself, but also by a respectful nod to the nearly two-hundred-year-old mill history that is personal to so many Biddeford area families. A museum, as well as walking tours geared to that history, is part of the project.

RESTORED MILL FLOOR, BIDDEFORD, MAINE.

"Some people call it the 'Biddesance,'" says Casavant, laughing and waving to a friend who's honked, as he and I walk along Main Street in the shadow of the mill complex. "But yes, the repurposing of the mills changed everything. I mean, if you'd told me just twenty years ago that the mills were going to be as they are now, diversified with all types of businesses and activities, I'd have looked at you like you were crazy."

"But like other cities, progress is a slog, right?" I ask, pointing to a couple of still-vacant storefronts. "You don't just banish boarded-up buildings overnight. How long for that to change more?"

"It's a process, for sure," he says over his shoulder, as he tests the lock on a door like a cop on the beat. "But we're so going in the right direction now. Biddeford today is the youngest city in the state of Maine, with a median age of thirty-five; young professionals who can't afford space in Portland are finding that here."

As if on cue, we round the corner onto Franklin Street, and there's the red, black, and gold gem that is the Palace Diner (see sidebar), saved and reopened by two Portland guys who'd been priced out of opening a place there. Cafés and bookstores have opened up, an arts and culture scene is burgeoning, exemplified by the ongoing rebirth of the City Theater. Built in 1896, it had fallen into disrepair and by the 1980s, its ground-floor orchestra section was being used to store piles of salt for the public works department.

"What I remember is, it was filthy dirty and it was painted like an army-surplus green."

Tim Sample recalls playing with his band, the Dubious Brothers, at the theater in the early 1970s. Since that time, Sample, an author and monologist, has become something of Maine's unofficial humorist laureate. And he's been back to perform here. On a rainy April afternoon, we're standing on the orchestra floor. Sample marvels at the now-gleaming theater's stunning rebirth, the success story of a city's deep support, and its refusal to lose this old but beloved building.

TIM SAMPLE, CITY THEATER, BIDDEFORD, MAINE. (BOB OLIVER)

PALACE DINER

(Biddeford, ME)

PALACE DINER, BIDDEFORD, MAINE.

You have to want to find the Palace Diner; you don't just spot a place that's at the end of a small one-way street and a municipal parking lot. 'Course, with only fifteen counter stools (no booths or tables), its regular customers are fine if you don't find it. The original dining car (1927) is Maine's oldest, but it finally closed during Biddeford's dark days. In 2014, two young Portland chefs, Chad Conley and Greg Mitchell, priced out of opening a place there, took a chance on reopening the diner.

"Hey, two guys, we kinda struck out in Portland, didn't have a lot of money, but we did have an idea," says Mitchell amid the chatter and din of a breakfast rush. "We just wanted to do breakfast and lunch, honest and tasty, and we kinda fell in love with this place from the start."

What they've pulled off is the single-hardest thing do with a diner: to tweak and elevate the simple "diner fare" that people expect, but do it subtly enough that the same dishes are all still there, just with a new twist or two.

"We call it the fine line between 'trash' and 'class,' nice touches, nothing fancy," says Mitchell. "We're just trying to do these classics justice."

Like . . . a whole new take on home fries, a tuna melt on challah bread, and pancakes that had a customer practically singing the Hallelujah Chorus at the counter. "Oh, my God," she practically whispered, in between bites. "Just the right fluffiness, a hint of lemon, wow."

Amazingly for a diner—any diner—even *Bon Appétit* magazine has joined the Palace fan club. None of which, fortunately, seems to have distracted the owners from what matters most with a diner. Any diner.

"The coolest thing about the diner has always been that everybody comes here," smiles Mitchell. "It's families, it's people going off to work in the morning, weekend adventures. My favorite is looking down the counter and seeing people—different ages, different parts of the country, different parts of the world—all enjoying the same thing."

"It's just so wonderful," Sample almost whispers, his head turning to take in the sweep of the hushed and ornate space, from balcony to stage. "People recognized that this was an integral part of the community. If not, this would be gone."

"The same goes for the mills across the street, too, no?" I ask.

"I love what's going on at the Pepperell Mills!" Sample says excitedly, clasping his hands together. "These disused spaces and the communities are reinventing themselves with a broader base than before, economically, demographically. We're coming back to them in new ways, and I love that. It's like we're looking at these spaces that are still here—theaters, mills, diners—and saying, 'Oh, look what we've always had, we've had it right here all along. Let's use it!'"

Reinventing. That's what many of these former New England mill towns are doing. Today, at the entrance to Biddeford's redeveloped Pepperell Mill complex, an inscription in Latin reads, "I Will Rise Again." And so a city has.

-⧸⧸⧸◆⧽⧽⧽-

Less than 20 miles north (Downeast!) of Biddeford is Maine's largest city, Portland.

Maine doesn't do big cities. (Hey, no one's coming to Vermont or New Hampshire for the nightlife, either.) A lot of Portland is bland and banged-up, making it basically Bangor with higher buildings and better restaurants. Then there's the Old Port.

It saves the city. (It's not saving anyone money; Portland's the most expensive place in Maine to live. Second-most expensive? *South* Portland.) There's plenty of new in the Old Port, but the old predominates, at least visually, and it's not tacky, it's not a put-on (i.e., it's not Fisherman's Wharf). It's still more or less real, and it works. You won't find that anymore on South Street in New York, or Baltimore's Inner Harbor, or anywhere on the entire Boston waterfront, for that matter. (The Hub's historic Fish Pier? Sold out for a corporate conference center.)

In fairness, it's not like Portland's Old Port has no shiny modern restaurants (too many) or glitzy boutique shops selling overpriced crap (way too many). But the bones of the old, working waterfront are still there. A chunk of the working waterfront is still working, and the rest hasn't been overly spruced up or prettified. Sure, every major hotel chain has crept in along the edges, and eventually the Old Port will be overrun. But for now, there are real working boats, real original brick waterfront buildings with real nineteenth-century dates on them.

There are original cobblestones on the streets. On Commercial Street, between the Peaks Island ferry and the Casco Bay Bridge, the counter at Becky's Diner is full before 8 a.m. It's controlled mayhem, and the attire varies from suits and nice shoes to stained sweatshirts and work boots. On some early mornings, you can catch a whiff of fish along with the coffee. I like the Old Port.

Portland is also the gateway to Maine's Midcoast area. Geographically, there are two things that make Maine famous: its ragged and rocky coastline, and its vast and forested interior. That signature ragged and rocky coastline—the stuff that makes you think of Maine—begins here, working its way Downeast. Small, lobster boat-studded harbors like Cundy's, Port Clyde, and Stonington. Long, narrow "finger peninsulas" that jut sharply into the Gulf of Maine at Pemaquid Point, Port Clyde, and further up at Blue Hill, Bass Harbor, and Brookline. And bigger inlets—with storied harbors like Rockland, Camden, and Castine, that in summer spread their sailboats like canvas confetti across the water.

Tougher to reach, but all the better to savor, are some of the legendary islands just off the Maine coast: Isle au Haut, Monhegan, Matinicus. Listening to the trio of Ann Mayo Muir, Gordon Bok, and Ed Trickett sing "Isle au Haut Lullaby" is like "seeing" with your ears what a Maine island looks like.

If the long (656 miles) and legendary drive up California's coastal Route 1 is a rite of passage, so, too, should be the drive up Maine's own coastal Route 1. Although marginally shorter overall (526 miles), it is far more meandering. (In fact, Maine's total "tidal shoreline," which includes its peninsulas, coves, inlets, and islands, measures longer—over 3,000 miles—than California's "general shoreline.") In Bristol, Maine, there's a plain, little white lighthouse that sits at the end of the long, finger peninsula that is Pemaquid Point. Seeing the sunrise at Pemaquid is breathtaking. But so is a summer fog. Or lightly falling snow in a chill December dusk. That's the thing about the Maine coast—it doesn't matter what the weather is. The ocean has its own personality, exerts its own identity on any given day in any season, in any light and any possible weather.

"I mean, look at it—we're fogged in, can't see twenty feet from the dock—and I love it!"

Bill Mangum and I are about to jump into his fourteen-foot wooden dory with a small outboard motor. A retired pilot from North Carolina, he and his wife moved to Harpswell, Maine, decades ago. Harpswell is a unique and fascinating place, more like a saltwater archipelago on the Maine coast. It's made up of the larger Harpswell Neck, which is connected to the mainland, plus a series of smaller finger peninsulas, as well as over two hundred small islands dotted

CUNDY'S HARBOR, HARPSWELL, MAINE. (BRIAN REITENAUER)

in, among, and offshore of the mainland's reaches. The largest of these islands—
Bailey, Orrs, and Great—connect to the mainland by bridges.

In their entirety, Harpswell's various outcroppings on the water account for
216 miles of coastline—the longest of any town in Maine. Cundy's Harbor is one
of the town's most enduringly authentic places.

"It's such a true Maine coast fishing village," says Mangum, tossing an extra
life vest into the boat ahead of my stepping in. "And this property's the heart and
soul of it."

The property is historic Holbrook's Wharf, where commercial fishing and
lobster boats have tied up since before the Civil War. The harbor is a long,
narrow sliver of inlet; the wharf lies at one end and it has, indeed, long been
the heart and soul of the area. A small general store sits above it and the local
school bus still turns around right in front of the store. But by 2005, times had
changed; fishing was tougher, but coastal property values in Maine had sky-
rocketed. The wharf's owners decided to put the property up for sale. Locals had
no doubt what was about to follow.

"First of all, and most importantly," says Mangum, "the local fishermen and
lobstermen would have never been able to repurchase that access here, 'cause
the access itself would have been gone."

"What was the likeliest outcome on the open market?" I ask.

"We wouldn't be standing here. Someone from out-of-state—pick your state—would have purchased this property. Prime spot for a hundred-foot yacht at the end of the dock, 'No Trespassing' sign, fences up. I mean, it's a gorgeous property."

But the Harpswell and Cundy's Harbor community hated the idea of losing what had for generations felt like *our* wharf, *our* place to head out to fish or lobster or just to say hello to a neighbor at the general store. So the community—those involved in fishing and lobstering, as well as those who had nothing to do with either—came together and tried to figure out what to do, how to save their wharf, their store, their place.

"We had our fits and starts getting going," Mangum says with a smile. "At one of the first community meetings, I made the mistake of raising my hand and asking, 'What is the business plan?' I'm also an accountant by training, so I asked what the business plan was for trying to save the property. And everybody goes, 'Business plan? What's a business plan? You're hired!'"

Plans did materialize. The Trust for Public Land stepped in to secure the property and take it off the market. The community fund-raised, putting its money where its memories and its meaning as a working waterfront were—the wharf. Today, they own it.

"We formed a 501(c)(3) nonprofit organization, the Holbrook Community Foundation, to acquire and manage the property," explains Mangum. "We rent out space on the dock, we rent the store as a means of income. We've kept it for the community."

The fog has lifted a bit as Bill Mangum and I tool slowly around the harbor, weaving in and around various larger fishing and lobster boats. A truck horn sounds on the shore nearby; an arriving lobsterman is getting out of his pickup, piled with traps in the back. He waves to Mangum, who waves back.

"So, it's actually working out here?" I ask. "Like, financially, it's working?"

"It really is. We have a mortgage we can manage, we've gotten good help from the state, and everyone here is on board—pun intended." Mangum laughs as he steers between the moorings of two classic Maine lobster boats. "Plus, there's a deed restriction now, so this will have to be commercial fishing forever. A hundred years from now, even if the foundation is gone, this property will be preserved for the community and for fishing."

Mangum throttles up a bit, his white wake widening behind us in the harbor as he makes a wide turn back in toward the dock. The fog has mostly dissipated. There are people moving about onshore and on boats, an activity that was shrouded in mist only minutes earlier. The lobsterman who waved is now wheeling some equipment from his truck down to the dock; a young kid, maybe his son, is helping him. A local bakery truck pulls in by the general store. Across the way at the little snack bar and ice-cream place above the wharf, two young women are laughing as they wipe off the outdoor picnic tables on the deck. Their laughter carries on the water, and Mangum smiles and points toward them.

"We have some old photographs of kids that same age, teenagers, offloading fish at that very dock."

It's a color image now. But it's continuity. I realize that what I'm really looking at is simply a somewhat updated scene that's essentially been the same for a very long time: local folks going about their day in and around the harbor, the heart and soul of their tight-knit community. And not a "Private Property" or "No Trespassing" sign in sight.

⤙⟨⟨⟨◆⟩⟩⟩⤚

Hard as it is to turn away from the Maine coast, there is, after all, a lot more to the state.

Like most larger states, Maine is defined by distinct geographic areas, with the most dramatic distinction being between its coastal and interior sections. Its interior, while less populated, is vastly larger than the coast. While nearly 45 percent of Maine's population (1.3 million) lives on the coast, those 144 coastal towns make up only 12 percent of the state's total area. Maine's interior, with its lakes, rivers, mountains, and deep pine forests, can be as storied and spectacular as its iconic seacoast. It's an immense inland area; it takes nearly six hours to drive the more than 350 miles between Kittery at the New Hampshire border in the south, and far northern Fort Kent along the Canadian border. Maine's southernmost York County, with its tourists and lobster stands, has little in common with northernmost Aroostook County, famous for its flat, open fields and potato farms. Known in Maine simply as "the County," Mainers rightly think of Aroostook as the state's "roof" and just generally being "way the hell up there." It is. As residents of the County are fond of saying, "It's not the end of the world—but you can see it from here."

Actually, you don't even need to get to within sight of world's end; northern Maine is so thinly populated, it's the end of towns themselves. One can drive for a hundred miles or more and, aside from the occasional logging truck blowing by, see literally nothing but trees. In fact, trees cover 88.8 percent of Maine, making it the nation's most forested state. In the early nineteenth century, led by native Abenaki guides, Henry David Thoreau made several trips here, writing about them in his book, *The Maine Woods*. Clearly, Thoreau was awed by the sheer, unending expanse of wild and untamed forest.

This was that Earth of which we have heard, made out of Chaos and Old Night. Here was no man's garden ... it was the fresh and natural surface of the planet Earth, as it was made for ever and ever—to be the dwelling of man, we say— so Nature made it, and man may use it if he can.

Man can, and has, used it ever since. Today, the enormous geographic area just south of Fort Kent is designated as the North Maine Woods. Made up of 155 unincorporated townships (numbered, not named), the NMW is mostly managed by a combination of public and private entities. Commercial logging is widespread; half a million acres of the state's forests are harvested annually.

To its credit, the state has also prioritized conservation and recreation, including in the North Maine Woods. The Allagash Wilderness Waterway is a nearly 93-mile-long protected ribbon of lakes, ponds, and streams, all more or less connected by the Allagash River. Established by the state of Maine in 1966, the Allagash extends from far northern Aroostook County down to the more central Piscataquis County, and is among the most famous and popular canoe routes in the United States.

Even further south in central Maine, the landscape is still heavily wooded and studded with lakes and ponds. In the Kennebec Valley region, little more than 10 miles north of the capital city of Augusta, the chain of seven lakes that comprise the Belgrade Lakes is spread out like giant daubs of bright blue amid the dappled green canvas of maple and pine. Just north of the lakes, I've enjoyed many long, summer afternoons with my kids, paddling around quiet Kimball Pond in tiny Vienna, Maine. (That's "VIGH-enna," locals will remind you.) The ragged, rocky coast may be the popular image of Maine, but boy, its woodsy, sprawling, lake-studded interior has a very, very special appeal, too.

KIMBALL POND, VIENNA, MAINE.

(From left) Auburn, Androscoggin River, Lewiston, Maine. (Haines Photography)

Thirty miles south of Augusta, you'll find L-A—minus the palm trees, freeways, and Hollywood Hills. The adjoining cities of Lewiston and Auburn are separated by the Androscoggin River, which in the nineteenth century powered the booming economies of both cities—shoes in Auburn, textiles in Lewiston.

As in Biddeford, and so many other former New England mill towns, it's the evolution and life cycle of Lewiston's mills that account for the evolution of the city itself. For well over a century, starting in the mid-1800s, the mills made Lewiston world-famous for textiles. Immigrants streamed to the city for work, including thousands and thousands of French Canadians, mostly from Quebec and New Brunswick. As with other mill towns like Lowell, Lawrence, and Biddeford, Lewiston's own "Petite Canada" left a large and lasting legacy. By the mid-twentieth century, French Canadian Americans made up 30 percent of Maine's population. Today, in Biddeford, and in the St. John Valley of Aroostook County (home to French speakers and Acadian culture), and particularly in Lewiston, Franco-American communities still thrive.

"*Bonjour, monsieur!*"

Rachel Desgrosseilliers is an older woman with short white hair, stylish big glasses, and one of those instant, incandescent smiles that makes you instantly and involuntarily smile, too.

Then the smile is gone and the hands come up. "*Faites attention, s'il vous plaît!* Please watch your step! We're setting up this new exhibit and there's a lot of stuff to trip on—I just did five minutes ago!"

Now retired, Desgrosseilliers served as executive director of Lewiston's Museum L-A (now Maine MILL), which preserves the rich history and culture of the city's working and immigrant communities. For Desgrosseilliers, it's a personal history in a personal setting. Her father worked as a weaver in the very same mill building that's now home to the museum.

"How does that feel," I wonder, "to be working in what was once a mill where your own dad worked?"

"Actually, the first time I was ever in this building, I was in my twenties, and I came in here because I always wondered why he came home with lint in his eyes, ears, nose. I mean, what goes on here?"

She turns to take in the whole, wide floor as she pauses to recall the details of that long-ago day.

"It was July when I came in. It was over a hundred degrees on the floor, humid. Dad was already mostly deaf because of the noise in there, and we were nose to nose, literally yelling to understand each other. And the lint was flying all over the place, and suddenly I understood what was going on."

"Wasn't easy work, was it?"

"For sure," she says, laughing. "Most of them had little education, they were hard workers, they helped their neighbors, and they built these communities. When I started here, we had a reunion for them; I told them this is a special day to honor you, the mill workers. And many said to me, 'Why? We're just mill workers.' And it was amazing to see after we talked to them and honored them, how their pride swelled up. Like, all of sudden, they were somebody—they were worth remembering."

She looks over at the wall next to her, carefully adjusts a pair of old work boots, one of dozens hanging on display.

"To be remembered, everyone who helped create this city's history," she says, turning back. "To me, that's what this museum is all about."

By the 1960s and '70s, the textile industry's retreat from Lewiston was nearly complete. What followed were more than twenty years of neglect, decay, and urban despair.

When I ask Desgrosseilliers about that period, she shakes her head slowly, as if trying to shake off a viscerally unpleasant sensation.

Bates Mill, Lewiston, Maine (c. 1960s). (Maine MILL)

"We were a mill town. These mills were the economic engines; the people who worked here knew they helped drive them. Then all of a sudden, overnight, that's gone. So as a community, we were nothing anymore, either."

"The identity is lost."

"The identity was lost completely," she says quietly, looking out the window. "It took a long time for us to get back from there."

Indeed, the 1970s and '80s were a tough time for Lewiston. Proud mill buildings that once hummed with noise and purpose sat dark and silent. But Lewiston, like Biddeford, slowly came back, with one mill after another being repurposed and redeveloped.

By 2000, Lewiston began seeing its newest immigrant wave: a rapid and swelling influx of immigrants from central and northern Africa, many of whom were refugees from the war and bloodshed in Somalia. There were difficult years of adjustment in Lewiston. The city was still finding its way back; resources were limited, tolerance was tested. The city's then-mayor made a disparaging remark about the increasing level of new immigration. Many felt the comments were not true to Lewiston's long history of immigration.

"When my parents and grandparents came down from Canada, they came down here to look for a better life for us, for their families," says Desgrosseilliers. "That's the same with the new immigrants. They want work. Just like we did."

Stores, businesses, cafés, and restaurants opened up in vacant buildings in block after block on Main Street and Lisbon Street. An empty storefront, vacant and off the tax rolls one day, suddenly sprouted a new sign—and taxes—the next: "Mogadishu Business Center." New languages were heard, new styles of clothing appeared. But the sense of industriousness and hard work was familiar.

In 2015, a story that caught national attention seemed to sum up the new era in Lewiston. A high school boys' soccer team went undefeated and won its first-ever state championship. The team included eight members whose families had fled a Somalian refugee camp in Kenya. In a documentary later, describing the team's first practice, then-coach Mike McGraw recalled seeing his returning players sitting at one end of the field, the new arrivals sitting at the other. "I went to both groups and said, Hey, I want you all to come over and sit in the middle," McGraw told the interviewer. "I sat one guy here, another guy there, all mixed in color. I said, 'This is how a team plays. Together. And this is how I want you to be on and off the field—together.'"

Lewiston isn't perfect. But it has battled back, and many here are justly proud of the fact that, through struggle and change, the city has continued to find coexistence, and community. As French Canadians and others once found a new beginning here, so now have many others, making Lewiston today Maine's most culturally diverse city.

"I'm a daughter of a mill worker, and proud of it," says Rachel Desgrosseilliers. "And there's another daughter out in this city today who looks different than me, but who's going to be proud of what her mother or father is doing to help build this city."

A1 DINER

(Gardiner, ME)

A1 DINER, GARDINER, MAINE. (MARK NICKLAWSKE)

The A1 Diner sits, appropriately, on Bridge Street. After all, it's the only diner I have ever seen (or heard of) that sits above a body of water—in this case, the Cobbosseecontee Stream, which flows off of the nearby Kennebec River. Walk down the stairs on the bridge to the stream itself, and sure enough, there are huge twenty-foot steel beams holding up the diner at street level.

"I would wager we're the only authentic Worcester diner in the world that exists like this," says owner Aaron Harris.

I'll take that bet. And the ham and cheese omelet with big, well-seasoned home fries. Although, have to say, even though it was only 8 a.m., I was tempted by the chicken sausage jambalaya. Or an avocado shrimp quesadilla. Not items you often see on a diner menu.

"Yeah, it used to be more of a greasy spoon, ashtray-on-the-counter kind of place you'd expect in the 1950s and '60s," Harris says, "but it's transitioned and evolved, and the menu has as well."

"Safe to say," I add, scanning the menu, "there was not a goat-cheese burger here in the fifties."

"I think that's safe to say," he says, nodding.

Harris has evolved and transitioned a bit himself. He used to work at the diner, left for a career in marketing, but the diner drew him back.

"I love cooking, but what I missed in marketing and the business world was that you don't feel like you have many opportunities to make people happy. Here—someone comes in, and in forty-five minutes you can make their day better!"

I watched it happen in real time. Local guy comes in, blank face, sits at counter, stares ahead. Coffee slides in, he looks up, Harris says, "Hey, great to see ya!" The guy breaks into a big smile. Twenty minutes later he can't decide whether to keep gobbling up his scrambled eggs or keep gushing to me about how great the place is.

"Been coming here for twenty-five years. Now that I'm retired, it's almost every day. And everything's good!"

Presumably, that's what Harris missed in his marketing days.

It's a friendly, cozy, classic yet unique diner that draws devoted locals as well as visitors. Nope, you won't find ashtrays on the counter anymore. But you will find a Moroccan roasted veggies and hummus wrap. *That's* evolution. Diner-style.

Ten miles west of Lewiston is the much smaller former mill town of Mechanic Falls. For the most part, unless you live there, you'd have little reason to follow State Route 121 for twenty minutes or so through Auburn and East Poland, Maine, to get to Mechanic Falls.

I had a good reason. And no trouble finding my destination, no GPS or Waze required. "Just stay on 121 till you hit the Silver Spur," I'd been told.

True enough. You just don't expect to see a fifteen-foot-high, silver boot spur by the roadside, resting on two green, steel cacti in the middle of Maine. But then, who'd expect a Maine Country Music Hall of Fame?

"I hear it all the time! Every visitor says, 'We had no idea there was something like this in Maine!'"

Yes, that's pretty much exactly what I said on an April afternoon in 2017 within minutes of being ushered inside by Slim Andrews.

"We're the only nonprofit hall of fame for country music northeast of Nashville."

"The only one."

"Only one," repeated Slim, his big, bony index finger pointing up in front of his lean face for emphasis. "They have halls of fame in Massachusetts, Rhode Island, and New Hampshire, but they have no museum or display, just a list of people."

The Maine Country Music Hall of Fame in Mechanic Falls consists of three large exhibit rooms under and attached to the Silver Spur, a local landmark country music and dance club. In 1978, Slim Andrews was one of the co-founders of Maine's Country Music Hall of Fame. He was also a longtime country music performer, guitarist, and songwriter. He's wearing a dark blue western shirt, big-buckled belt, and a nifty, tan ten-gallon. He's in his mid-eighties, but thin and sprightly as he darts about, pointing out music memorabilia. Hats, boots, records, sheet music, photos, guitars. They fill display cases, and are laid out on tables; they cover the walls, and hang from the ceiling.

SLIM ANDREWS, MECHANIC FALLS, MAINE.

"This fiddle here is handmade," Slim says, running his hand gently in the air over it. "Played by the best fiddle player ever to come out of Maine, Lucky Tim Farrell. And by the way—Lucky was his real name."

Slim points at a corner. "See that banjo? Bob French made that. And boy, he and his wife Grace, great bluegrass people."

Slim motions for me to follow him.

"Lemme show you something," he says over his shoulder as we go around a corner into another room. "See that piece of board on the wall, with the 45 on it?" asks Slim. "That's an original, 1965, first-issue Dick Curless, 'A Tombstone Every Mile.'"

Known for his eye patch and deep voice, Dick Curless remains Maine's most famous country star, with more than twenty hit recordings. His most famous, "A Tombstone Every Mile," refers to the countless deaths of truckers on the long, straight, lonely highway connecting far northern Aroostook County with the rest of Maine. Not for the first time, as Slim and I walk about the rooms, I'm struck all over again by how incongruous this whole country music thing seems—the cowboy hats, embroidered suits, hand-tooled boots—right here in the heart of lumbering, lobstering, and L.L.Bean.

"I mean, you have to admit, Slim," I say, palms up before me, "unless you've been involved in it, been exposed to it, most people just don't associate a rich country music history with Maine."

"Oh, I get it, I know it," says Slim, smiling and shaking his head with the polite, practiced cadence of someone who's said these very words, tilted his head this very way, many, many times before. "First thing to tell you—Maine is one of the largest contributors to country music in the entire country. Now that's a fact."

Slim Andrews is, hands down, one of the nicest, sweetest people I have ever met in my life. But I doubted that "fact" very much. Even as he said it, I found myself mentally ticking off a quick half-dozen states well south of Maine that produced country music legends known from Bangor to Boise. While Slim took a quick phone call, my mental list grew to well over a dozen states.

But know what? Doesn't matter. I realized I was heartily eating up this unexpected and unknown (to me) part of Maine. Who cares if Dick Curless wasn't Patsy Cline, that Lucky Time Farrell wasn't Hank Williams, or that Bob and Grace French weren't Johnny Cash and June Carter? They were from places like Fort Fairfield, Maine, not Fort Worth, Texas, and that made their legitimate contribution to country music that much more unlikely and remarkable. I was equally delighted by Slim himself; his passion, his detailed knowledge. His warm, earnest desire to share it all was infectious. And share he did.

"In the late 1930s, WABI radio in Bangor started broadcasting the 'Lone Pine Mountaineer,' which was picked up and could be heard in California."

"Originated in Maine?"

"Yes, sir—originated right here in Maine."

"But where, Slim," I wonder aloud, "did this interest in country music begin and get fed here in Maine?"

"Well, I'll tell ya—one big influence was that WWVA, the big radio station in Wheeling, West Virginia, had a 50,000-watt clear station, and all we could get up here in Maine for country music was WWVA. And everybody listened to it."

"Still, you must have run into that all around the country, right?" I ask. "There must be people who wonder, how's a guy from Maine a country music performer, right?"

"Yeah, all the time, and I say, really, it's pretty simple—when I was eight years old, my dad bought me an old crystal radio set with the earphones, and I'd fall asleep listening to Lee Moore, the coffee-drinking nighthawk from Wheeling's WWVA!"

Another fun fact? Slim Andrews is not Slim Andrews.

Leonard Andrew Huntington was born in Boston in 1931. When he was six months old, his family moved to Auburn, Maine.

"How'd 'Slim' come about, Slim?" I ask.

"By the time I was actually performing, I was five-eleven and a hundred and fifty pounds soaking wet. My name didn't seem so country for me. You know, Harold Jenkins felt the same way, so he changed it to 'Conway Twitty.' I changed it to Slim Andrews."

He made a career in insurance to support his family, which included six children. He'd move about to different companies, in Michigan, Georgia, all the while performing regularly wherever he was.

"I could've played bigger places, but you have to live. I never had much respect for someone who had children and took off and left his wife and kids home and went to Nashville and tried to make it."

He made it in his own way, family and all. He made five records in his career, and figures he's written twenty-five to thirty songs, which consistently get air play on country outlets everywhere. He has performed all over the world, and in 2002 was himself inducted into the Maine Country Music Hall of Fame.

"So this is the Slim Andrews corner of the Hall," I say, smiling.

Slim is standing back a bit, while I look about the collection of his memorabilia.

"They got your boots, a guitar, couple of your hats, your CDs," I say as I turn to him. He's smiling. "This must be nice to see your stuff in the Hall of Fame, huh?"

"You better believe it," he says softly.

Slim kept up a regular performing schedule into his early eighties. At eighty-five, he had recently performed his last public concert in Bangor.

"An old grange hall there that catered to country music," he says. "We held the homeless veterans show there for many years."

"You gonna miss it?"

"Yeah, sure. But when people are paying to see a show, they have a right to expect it's gonna be worth it. And when you can't remember the lines to a song that you wrote yourself, well, that's a problem."

One of Slim's songs is called "Born to Win." But there was plenty of loss, too. He buried three of his children, lost two wives, and fought cancer himself several times, including throat cancer.

"Everyone has loss," he says, while idly running his fingers over the strings on an old guitar of his. "I'll tell you what, though—my youngest son, he's a hell of a songwriter. I've even recorded a song of his."

"So, he's continuing the tradition."

"Yes, he is. He's writing, plays a bit of guitar, but his love is writing country music. And, oh, boy, he's good."

We started wrapping up, kept chatting while Slim went from room to room turning off lights. He kept apologizing that he had to leave, had to head home to tend to his ailing wife.

"Come back during the summer," he said as we shook hands. "We'll have some live music, you'll hear some of these talented folks."

I told him that sounded like fun. I knew I'd likely not make it back. That doesn't lessen what I felt when I was there. It was one of the most special afternoons I'd ever spent. Anywhere. And I wasn't sure why. Was it because the Maine Country Music Hall of Fame represented something so unique, so off the beaten path, and so unlike the Maine I thought I knew, and that I genuinely learned something new and wonderful?

Or was it because all of that came courtesy of a lovely old gentleman in a cowboy hat who seemed of a different era entirely, and whose simple, soft-spoken genuineness impressed me deeply?

I decided it was both.

Later on, I downloaded some Slim Andrews songs, listening to them occasionally when I wanted a lift. As I was writing this, in April of 2023, I decided to check in on Slim, who, by my reckoning, would have been ninety-one. I learned that he had died just about a year earlier.

I never did make it back to Mechanic Falls. But boy, I'm glad I got there when I did.

—≺≺≺◆≻≻≻—

CHAPTER 6

Into the Whites, onto the Roof

Leaving Maine through its western mountains means coming into another region of New England with its own particular appeal: the White Mountains of New Hampshire, and the Mount Washington Valley.

Route 302 through Fryeburg, Maine, passes into Conway, New Hampshire, a pretty town of ten thousand or so, ringed by mountains. But the more interesting history begins just 5 miles north, in Conway's largest village, North Conway.

First, the downside: Routes 302 and 16 as they enter North Conway suddenly spread out into an appalling mess of malls and outlet shopping that seems as out of place in this mountain setting as a McDonald's in the middle of a mountain meadow. Which is kind of what it is.

The upside? It ends. The chain stores slip away, the view is freed. To the left in the distance, the rocky prominence of Cathedral Ledge. In the near distance, the lovely town green, and at the far end, looking like a cross between a gingerbread house and a Disneyland transplant, is the very real, very Victorian, and very yellow and red train station. A local landmark since 1874, only the local Conway Scenic Railroad rolls through and uses the station today.

At one time the station teemed, especially with skiers. Beginning during the Great Depression years of the 1930s, the Boston & Maine Railroad began running weekend ski trains from Boston's North Station up to North Conway, New Hampshire. By the late 1940s, trains were running from Grand Central Station in New York, too. Every winter weekend, thousands of skiers would head up to the slopes of North Conway's Cranmore Mountain, as well as other fabled early ski towns in New England, like Franconia, New Hampshire, and Woodstock and Stowe in Vermont.

SNOW TRAIN ARRIVING IN N. CONWAY, 1940S. (COLLECTION OF DWIGHT A. SMITH)

One of the most famous skiers to have stepped off a train in North Conway was Hannes Schneider. In the 1930s, Schneider was already a pioneering figure in the growing sport of skiing, having created his famous ski school in the Arlberg region of the Austrian Alps. He was also an outspoken critic of the Nazis. After Germany annexed Austria in 1938, the ski school was shut down and Schneider was imprisoned. American businessman and Cranmore Mountain Resort's founder, Harvey Gibson, was able to secure Schneider's release and bring him and his young family to New Hampshire, to transplant his famous ski school to Cranmore Mountain Resort.

Later, during World War II, Schneider was instrumental in helping to develop and train the famed Tenth Mountain Division. In the Mount Washington Valley, Schneider, like the famous von Trapp family (fellow Austrians who also escaped the Nazis, settling in Stowe, Vermont), was reminded of home. To be sure, St. Anton and the Tyrol are rarely confused with North Conway and the White Mountains. But the snow-dotted winter peaks of the Presidential Range are stunning, and the tallest one would certainly have appeared Alp-like to Schneider.

At 6,288 feet, Mount Washington dominates the valley below it. It's the Northeast's highest mountain, and the most topographically prominent mountain east of the Mississippi River. But what really sets the summit of Mount Washington apart is not height, but wind. On April 12, 1934, the Mount Washington Weather Observatory recorded a wind speed of 231 miles per hour. It remains the highest wind speed ever measured not connected with a tornado or cyclone. Yes, you can hike,

ALPENGLOW, MOUNT WASHINGTON. (ART DONAHUE)

drive, or ride a train up it. You can get snacks at the top, take a few pictures, buy New England's most ubiquitous bumper sticker (THIS CAR CLIMBED MT. WASHINGTON), and head back down. But being at the top in nice weather gives no sense whatsoever of what life on the "roof of New England" is like in its more typical state: horrible weather. In winter, the year-round meteorological staff on the summit works in conditions that include hurricane-force winds, ice, fog, drifting snow, and wind chills of easily 50-below.

Working on Mount Washington is one thing. Playing on it in winter and spring can be far more lethal. Since the mid-1800s, nearly two hundred people have died on the mountain. Winter climbers get lost, disoriented, or disappear into elevator shaft–like crevices, their bodies to be recovered, with luck, months later. In spring, in the mountain's legendary Tuckerman Ravine, there is constant avalanche danger; melting ice chunks the size of small cars often break off and tumble half a mile down its slopes.

Adding to these dangers are the mountain's frequent and precipitous weather changes. My own first experience hiking up the roughly 4 miles to ski Tuckerman Ravine was many years back, on a Memorial Day. At midmorning, the temperature at the mountain's base was around 55 degrees. After a few runs, sitting on the famous "lunch rocks" in the bright afternoon sun, the temperature had climbed to nearly 68. Then a front approached. The skies darkened, the wind picked up, the air chilled, and it began to spit freezing rain. Heading hurriedly back down the now-slickened trail, the freezing rain had turned to flurries. The temperature had plummeted nearly 30 degrees in less than three hours. Mount Washington is not to be trifled with.

MOUNT WASHINGTON, TUCKERMAN'S RAVINE (FAR LEFT), PINKHAM NOTCH, NEW HAMPSHIRE.
(ART DONAHUE)

As fearsome and forbidding as Mount Washington can be up close and on it, it's instead a striking image to behold in the distance from miles—even hundreds of miles—away. Its prominent peak and stark flanks can be snow-topped for more than half the year, making the mountain visible, from the right vantage points, even in neighboring states.

But the entire valley is draped in equally arresting beauty. The Presidential Range presents a cascade of ridges that nearly rival Washington itself; Mount Adams and Mount Jefferson are just under six thousand feet. It's a breathtaking landscape, at turns force-of-nature wild, and languidly pastoral, all sculpted fifteen thousand years ago by the massive, moving hand of the last retreating ice sheet. Rocky peaks jutting into the clouds, rolling mountainsides that plunge thousands of feet down to the shadowed valley floor where, in spring, snow-swollen rivers and streams fork and forge through the dense green pines and firs of a national forest. There is a keen, signature scent of balsam here that is so prevalent, so pure and powerful, that even if I smell it on a candle in some distant gift shop, I can close my eyes and instantly be transported to the North Country of New Hampshire. Just as the European Alps in the eighteenth and nineteenth centuries drew poets and painters, composers and philosophers awed and inspired by their natural beauty, so did the White Mountains. They still do.

"Within forty-five minutes of this spot, I can go to a very pastoral and peaceful farmland landscape, or I can drive up into Pinkham Notch where I can have just an incredible, dramatic rocky, wild experience."

Erik Koeppel is one of those artists. He's lived in the White Mountains since he was ten. He'd always wanted to paint. He trained, worked, and lived in New York for a while, but was drawn back to the mountains.

"I just started feeling like—why am I leaving to go paint in the city for the winter? So I came back. For good. Something about it really speaks to me, I guess."

Koeppel's studio is in Jackson, New Hampshire, a small and quintessential mountain town, just about exactly halfway up Route 16 between North Conway and Mount Washington. When we met, he was in his late thirties, with dark, uncombed hair, deep, dark eyes, and a certain restrained energy that revealed itself in the passion with which he spoke about his art, painting, and this valley.

"There are lots of places with bigger mountains, and other places with farm country, but there's not a lot of places where all these things are sort of intermingled in this wild way, and form these incredible backgrounds and landscapes."

An accomplished traditional landscape painter, Koeppel today is a leading figure in the revival of both the techniques and the philosophy behind the famed Hudson River and White Mountains schools of art.

"If you read Thoreau or Emerson, they were trying to point out the importance of spiritual thought, and reflection, contrasted against how they perceived industrialization in the nineteenth century, really, you know, destroying that part of life. This was a place—the mountains here—that spoke to them, and that inspired painters, too, and their paintings just expressed this beautiful human sentiment through landscape. I fell in love with that."

Erik Koeppel. (Erik Koeppel)

In the same way that the original nineteenth-century Hudson River School artists were influenced by eighteenth-century Romanticism, so do Koeppel's paintings reflect those same themes. They seem to powerfully, reverently echo that earlier, classic landscape style. A spring scene stands out: greening meadow, wildflowers sprouting among huge rocks, and past the dense pines, the soaring, spreading silver flanks of Mount Washington, still holding its gleaming white snowpack, its summit almost an ethereal presence above it all.

I found myself fascinated by these works—the rich detail, the painterly skill, the precision of place, the passion that underlay it all. I questioned Koeppel about his technique, his process.

He never uses photographs. "If I felt that photographs were going to improve the work, I would use them. I go outside with my easel and I have this experience in nature, and by having that, over an extended period of time, I feel like I get a deeper knowledge of the subject. And when I'm back in the studio with it, I feel like then I'm free to use my imagination. It was more difficult at first, but as you keep practicing it gets easier."

Koeppel and I stand and chat for a bit outside on the back deck of his studio. It's a cloudy fall morning, the air is cool and clean, the surrounding woods, still lush with full but changing leaves.

"Safe to say you have a real reverence for where you are here?" I ask.

"Very much so. I loved it here even as a little kid, loved the beautiful landscape, knew it was special. But I wasn't necessarily aware of the tradition of painting here. Now I feel a part of that."

—◄◄◄◆►►►—

From Pinkham Notch, it's 15 miles back down 16 to Conway, and a sharp right onto Route 112, which is far better known by its other name, the Kancamagus Highway. ("The Kanc," to locals.) Kancamagus, grandson of the legendary chief, Passaconaway, was a Native American leader of the Penacook Confederacy who bitterly fought the advance of English settlers in the late 1600s. Today, the 35-mile scenic highway runs east-west through the heart of the White Mountain National Forest. Part of it is closed in winter, and in summer its beauty can be obscured if one is crawling behind a slow-moving parade of cars, buses, and Winnebagos. At nearly three thousand feet, the narrow, two-lane roadway curves and weaves past waterfalls that seem to sprout in places mere feet from the roadway.

The entire length is dotted with trailheads; an expansive network takes hikers deep into the woods and high into the Presidentials. Turnouts offer sweeping, panoramic views across the valley. As a kid, I loved camping trips along the Kanc, hiking up to ice-cold, crystal-clear mountain ponds, and swimming at Lower Falls. From its western exit in Lincoln, it also usually meant a side trip a few miles north to Franconia, where soaring 4,080-foot Cannon Mountain looms over the notch there. Its own celebrated ski history aside, the mountain's south-facing side was long famous for the "Old Stone Face," a natural rock profile made up of a series of cliffs and ledges that together, if viewed from a certain angle far below, unmistakably resembled the stern and chiseled visage of a man. Indeed, the "Old Man of the Mountain" came to be the identifying face, symbol, and granite embodiment of New Hampshire. Then, in May 2003, he was gone. Alas, just as naturally occurring rockslides had created the profile eons ago, so the same rockslides eventually took it down. He is missed.

Below Franconia, it's a steady drive south into central New Hampshire and its Lakes Region. Just north of Concord (the state capital), Interstate 93 intersects with State Route 4, which connects Concord with Portsmouth and the seacoast, about 45 miles to the east. By the 1970s, this section of Route 4 (also officially known as "First New Hampshire Turnpike") was popularly referred to as "Antique Alley." It's often said that New Hampshire's Route 4 has the highest concentration of antiques shops on one contiguous thoroughfare in America. Why so many antiques shops on this one stretch of road? Beats me. I've never entirely figured it out. But I've asked others.

"Well, it's a brutal commute from Concord to Portsmouth on Route 4," says Colleen Pingree. "You're driving in traffic through all these tiny towns, behind trucks, and for most of the time it's only a two-lane road."

"You realize," I say in response, "that based on your description of this road, no one will ever want to come here again."

Pingree throws her head back and laughs. "No, I mean, you feel like you have to stop! So all these antiques shops help you keep your sanity as you drive the road."

I suppose it's as good a theory as any. They certainly continue to stop at Pingree's shop, R. S. Butler's Trading Company in Northwood, which she runs with her husband, Don. For one thing, it's become a local landmark over the decades they've had it, partly because it's painted a very deep shade of purple. It's located at the top of a slight rise on Route 4, just ahead of an intersection and stoplight.

Pingree isn't sure if that helps or hurts.

"Cars are sometimes backed up at that light for half a mile or more in front of our shop. We can never decide if that's helpful because people are looking at us longer, or if it's problematic because they're like, My God, I need to make that light—I can't stop!"

"I guess that could go either way."

"Exactly! Who knows?"

What I do know is that, regardless of the traffic light, Colleen and Don Pingree have become a must-stop for me on Route 4 over the years. Not only are they an uncommonly sweet and funny couple, but they've also become sort of the unofficial "deans" of Antique Alley.

"Wacky and whimsical" would best describe R. S. Butler's. Also, "overstuffed." The shop takes up the entire ground floor of an old Victorian home; Don and Colleen live upstairs. The couple's huge, brown Newfie sits placidly on the porch, barely roused by the frequent foot traffic in and out. Inside is a warren of rooms, all loosely themed—small stuff, big stuff, weird stuff. The 1950s and '60s are well represented, and scattered throughout, genuine century-old antiques as well. Fact is, though, antiques stores themselves are becoming something of an antique. They've certainly dwindled here on Antique Alley.

R. S. BUTLER'S, ANTIQUE ALLEY, NORTHWOOD, NEW HAMPSHIRE.

"In terms of the number of shops, we're about half of what we were in the heyday," says Pingree, as we stand outside in the welcome warm sun of a late fall afternoon. "Antiques shops that I used to go to, they don't exist anymore. People age out, they close their shops."

"Not many younger people to take them over, right?"

"Almost never now," she adds.

"But you guys have hung in."

"We love this life. Don and I have two friends who work two days a week for us. What do we do those two days? We're out looking for stuff! So yeah, it's a way of life. It's an obsession. But a healthy obsession!"

<hr />

Northwood, in New Hampshire's Rockingham County (the state's oldest), is not a large town—just under five thousand people. It's got a couple of decent-sized lakes and a very pretty state park. It's also home to one of my favorite—and more importantly, funniest—New Englanders. On a drive down Route 4 in the fall of 2021, in addition to checking in at R. S. Butler's, I also checked in at Rebecca Rule's house. Even better, it was the first stop of the day. As a pick-me-up, the coffee was mere overkill.

"Let me show you the new COVID chickens!" she says excitedly, leading us around back. "We waited all winter for them to lay, but now we have the best eggs. Aren't fresh eggs the best?"

The small chicken coop in the backyard was indeed new since our last visit.

"Hey—we were all *cooped* up here, anyway!" She laughs in her way.

Becky Rule says a lot of very funny things. But she doesn't actually laugh at them. Or rather, she *seems* to be laughing. She has this broad smile that involves her whole round face; she smiles a toothy grin, her nose crinkles a bit, her glasses lift a bit, and you, the listener, end up breaking into a laugh. Which she clearly enjoys immensely. It's like tickling a person. Which is kind of what Becky Rule does. And in her dozen or so books all about New

REBECCA RULE, NORTHWOOD, NEW HAMPSHIRE.
(SCHUYLER D. SCRIBNER)

England culture and customs, in her popular talks, she knows exactly where the most ticklish spots are.

"New Englanders, you know," she says, seemingly apropos of nothing, as she gathers up some eggs in a small basket, "they can get very touchy about who's a native in their town. You can be a 'newcomer' for a long, long time."

"So when," I ask, "are you no longer the newcomer in an old New England town?"

"When the last person who knows when you moved there *dies*, congratulations—you're a native!"

Rebecca Rule loves the colorful and plentiful peculiarities of small-town New Englanders. Especially the language. In her book, *Headin' for the Rhubarb*, she compiled a glossary of obscure New Hampshire terms like, well, "headin' for the rhubarb."

"Horses, if they eat rhubarb, it's bad for them, makes 'em sick," Rule says, as we sit in the sun at a small table behind her house. "So if you see a hoss that's heading for the rhubarb, you want to pull that hoss back. You can say that about anybody who's getting up to some trouble—'Oh, boy, she's headin' for the rhubarb.'"

My favorite term? *Adeldufia*. Nope, not a place.

"So, you go into Calef's Country Store over in Barrington, and you put your goods on the counter and Tina behind the counter says, 'Adeldufia?'"

"In other words, 'Will that do for you?'"

"Yup! But why use five words when one word'll do it!"

The quintessential thrifty Yankee. Even with words.

The mention of Calef's Country Store gets Rule and me talking about a couple of our favorite New England institutions—general stores and town meetings. In her book, *Moved and Seconded*, she wrote about the institution that is the New England town meeting. She lauds it as one of the few remaining public political activities that is, by design, entirely nonpartisan.

"Everyone uses the road that needs paving," I agree. "Who cares what party you vote for?"

"Town meeting and country stores—two of the most iconic New England traditions," Rule says, laying her hand down flatly on the table for emphasis. "And we do not want to lose either one if we can help it."

"Iconic and beloved, yes, but let's face it, Becky—both are threatened. More and more."

"Both are threatened, yes, maybe the stores more so. Thankfully, we still have Calef's!"

"And Joel!" I chime in.

"And Joel Sherburne, yes!* And thankfully, two-thirds of towns here in New Hampshire still have traditional town meeting, and I hope they hold."

"Tougher and tougher to sell participation, though," I say. "Takes time. You gotta be there, you gotta show up."

"Makes me sad," she says. "People say things like"—affecting a whine—"'It's *hard.* I don't like people knowing how I *vote.*' Well, guess what? Democracy is hard. It's messy and it's hard."

We sit a bit more. We both know that both institutions are living relics. (We don't acknowledge that maybe that's a bit of what we are, too.)

We head into the house. I say hello to Becky's husband, John, who seems to be fixing some small appliance, working intently at the kitchen table. In her book-lined study, Rule sits down at her desk and describes her current book project. It's a departure in some ways: a murder mystery. Naturally, it's set in a small New England town, filled with interesting, quirky, New England characters.

But the author is in a bit of a predicament. "I can't decide which one to kill off!"

"But it's a murder mystery," I say, picking up a large, wooden gavel from a shelf, given to Rule at some town meeting somewhere. "So some unlucky someone's gonna have to buy it, right?"

"I suppose," she says with a frown. "But the more I write about them, the more I really like them. I like them *all.* I don't want to kill anyone off!"

I suspect Becky Rule should have set her murder mystery somewhere other than New England.

---

*Joel Sherburne is a legendary figure at Calef's Country Store in Barrington, New Hampshire. He began working at the store in the 1950s, and was still Calef's cheese-cutter in 2020. In 2017, Rule celebrated Sherburne in her book, *Sixty Years of Cuttin' the Cheese: Joel Sherburne and Calef's Famous Country Store.*

RED ARROW DINER

(Manchester, NH)

RED ARROW DINER, MANCHESTER, NEW HAMPSHIRE. (ANNE-MARIE DORNING)

There's been a Red Arrow Diner on Manchester's Lowell Street since 1922, when enterprising David Lamontagne opened its doors to serve the hordes of mill and factory workers looking for a hot meal at odd hours. Today, the mills and factories are gone, but the diner is still open 24/7, and is a Manchester landmark.

The original Lowell Street location (there are now three others) is still small, with an interior "L" shape, the main counter area connecting to a small grouping of tables and chairs next to the front windows. The food is good, the portions are big (the blue plate specials are served on blue plates), the desserts are very fattening. (The venerable Twinkie lives again as the Red Arrow's "Dinah Fingers.") It's cozy, friendly, with legions of regulars, but perhaps the Red Arrow is most famous for the unique group who drop in only once every four years.

Given New Hampshire's traditional early presidential primary, the diner has long been an obligatory stop for any and all US presidential candidates. Owner Carol Lawrence won't tell you who she's voted for, but she's happy to share memories of what the candidates eat when they stop by. Some years back, she's pretty sure Hillary Clinton had a tuna melt. But she's definitely sure about Bill Richardson: "He had two orders of bacon! Two orders!" For the record, I've generally stuck to a ham and cheese omelet, home fries, wheat toast, side of hash. Only one order.

Back to Concord, and a straight shot, 18 miles down Interstate 93 South toward Manchester, the state's most populous city (110,229). For a proud old mill town once down on its luck, Manchester's had a bit of a revival. The city deserves it, too. I'm good with a lunch stop at the landmark Red Arrow Diner (see sidebar), before heading southwest on NH Route 101, which winds through Hillsborough County, passing lovely little southern New Hampshire towns like Mont Vernon (great little general store), Amherst, and Milford. Just 5 miles or so farther west is the small, unassuming, mostly wooded town of Wilton. Once a textile mill town (at the confluence of the Souhegan and Stony Brook rivers), today it has a population of around 3,600, and is mostly a bedroom community for the larger surrounding cities of Manchester, Nashua, and even northern Massachusetts.

Wilton feels very rural, but one patch of woods stands out above the others. Literally.

"This one is easily over 150 feet, maybe 175," says Swift Corwin.

"And how old?" I ask, looking straight up, tilting my head as far back as it goes.

"Probably two hundred to two hundred and fifty years old."

"And there are older trees than this here."

"Oh, yeah, there are some that are over three hundred and fifty years old."

"Holy shit."

Less than thirty minutes from an interstate highway and the state's second-largest city tower two-hundred-foot-tall trees that predate the American Revolution. All of which makes the Sheldrick Forest Preserve in Wilton something of a modern-day marvel: an existing old-growth forest in the midst of a modern-day, highly developed area. Sometimes called "virgin" or "primeval forests," these places are defined as extensive stands of woods or whole forests "that have attained great age without significant disturbance."

Needless to say, they are exceedingly rare in highly populated and developed areas like southern New Hampshire. On a chilly early-November afternoon, I'm admiring these huge trees with Corwin, a professional forester. A sturdy, six-foot-plus, late-forty-something guy in a stocking cap, plaid wool jacket, and jeans, Corwin leads us further down the forest trail, descending along a wooded hillside as we do. Without breaking stride, he points off to the right just ahead of us.

"The *real* oldies," he says over his shoulder.

I keep following behind. The trail narrows and levels off; we're at the bottom of a steep ravine in the woods. Corwin stops, spreads his arms in a circling motion as if to say, "Voila." Indeed, on the sides of the ravine, which we're now standing at the bottom of, are massive red oaks, white pines, hemlock, and beech trees. The tallest ones seem even taller now, as some are standing a good forty or fifty feet up the side of the ravine.

Looking up toward the sky and the tree canopy, I turn my head, shuffling my feet to make a full circle where I stand. It's quiet and still, save for some wind in the high branches and an occasional bird. It feels cathedral-like. I'm reminded of standing in the lush, green Muir Woods of Northern California, staring up at giant old-growth redwoods. I laugh out loud at the thought. Corwin finds it funny, too.

"I mean, it kind of astounds me," I say, "this close to Nashua."

"Crazy, right?"

"So what accounts for the fact that these huge trees, this close to an urban area, have stayed here this long and have never been forested?"

"There's patches here that were just really hard to get to," Corwin says. "I mean, this ravine—it was hard to find and hard to get into. It would have been brutal to timber in here and get trees this size out. So they were remnant, they were just left alone, and that's the most amazing thing."

Not quite.

By the late-twentieth century, these woods were not left alone. The property had passed from the longtime owners, the Sheldrick family. The new owner hired a forestry team to inventory and tag trees in preparation for both large-scale logging and land development.

Swift Corwin headed that team.

"Our job was to mark this whole forest for harvest," Corwin says, recalling that week about twenty years earlier. "I've been on a lot of pieces of land. I've done a lot of timber inventories. And right from the start here, I was struck—the natural diversity, the volume, the age of the trees, how undisturbed it all was. It wasn't just me; we all felt it, me and the other two guys. And as we're marking, we started to feel worse and worse about it. This was something special, something remarkable and rare."

"Just the same, you were hired to prepare it all to be cut down."

"Yes, we were. And toward the end of that week, my colleagues and I were sitting on the leaves eating our lunch, and I said, we have to do something."

"You felt like it had to be saved."

"Yeah, no question. We all did."

'Course, the land wasn't Swift Corwin's to save, or not save. He first went to the landowner.

"I tried to express to him that this was, in fact, a very special place, and that the undisturbed nature of it was really the thing that made it so special."

The landowner was receptive to talking further, and Corwin realized he had an opening. He reached out to a contact at the Nature Conservancy of New Hampshire. Although the Nature Conservancy has acquired, preserved, and manages natural resources in countries across the globe and in all fifty American states, it had never heard of the Sheldrick Forest. Nor, as they learned, were most people around the forest in New Hampshire familiar with what made the woods remarkable.

SWIFT CORWIN, SHELDRICK FOREST PRESERVE, WILTON, NEW HAMPSHIRE. (BOB OLIVER)

The Nature Conservancy quickly made sure that changed. By engaging the local community and drawing widespread local support for a preservation effort, the Nature Conservancy was able to persuade the landowner to sell the property. Today, the Sheldrick Forest Preserve is owned by the Nature Conservancy. It comprises 227 acres, with 3 miles of hiking trails, all open to the public.

"People love these woods," Corwin says. "I mean, they always liked that they were here, but it had been private property, and even local folks didn't really understand how unique it was."

It's late afternoon, the light fading fast, as Swift Corwin and I spend a few final minutes talking in the chill hush of the woods, admiring the slanting shafts of brilliant gold slicing down between the towering trees to the forest floor hundreds of feet below.

"You know, I never want to feel like a hypocrite, because I made my living my whole career, for almost forty years, cutting down trees," says Corwin, his arms folded, looking out in the near distance. "I'm guilty of cutting a lot of woods in the world. I am."

"But not these."

"Not these," he says, shaking his head, then looking around us. "It's amazing to be here—what, twenty, twenty-five years later—still talking about that week. I can still point out trees that we'd tagged, trees that'd be long gone now."

I watch out of the corner of my eye as Corwin slowly runs his hand over the speckled brown bark of a huge white pine. "You feel pretty special about this forest."

"Yes," he says, nodding, looking up to the canopy high above. "I do."

—«««◆»»»—

From Wilton, 101 West winds into southwestern New Hampshire and Cheshire County. The road here undulates through the rolling hills of the Monadnock Region, weaving through wonderful, historic towns like Peterborough, Dublin, Hancock, and Harrisville.

The highest point in Cheshire County, in Jaffrey, is a solo affair. It shares company with no surrounding ridges, no neighboring mountains. It rather seems to just spring skyward whole, a single large, rising mass of woods and rocky crown with the sky all to itself. Which, geologically speaking, is pretty much exactly what a "monadnock" is. And indeed, Mount Monadnock—3,166 feet with no other peak near it—towers over the region and seems to be ever-present. Even when it dips from view.

"It plays hide-and-seek. You find yourself looking for it, then you go around the bend, suddenly there it is. You look across the pond, there it is. So, it's always with you, but it chooses its moment to show itself to you."

Howard Mansfield lives just north of Jaffrey in Hancock, New Hampshire. A prolific author, he writes about history, preservation, and architecture. Over the years, I've met up many times with Howard, whether it was talking about New England's iconic meeting houses, covered bridges, or the fascinating legacy of the Shakers. His 2006 book, *Where the Mountain Stands Alone: Stories of Place in the Monadnock Region*, looks at how, over centuries, people have interacted with this unique mountain.

On a brilliantly clear mid-October morning, we're standing on a grassy hillside on the edge of a two-hundred-year-old cemetery in little Dublin, New Hampshire. Facing us a short distance below is glassy-blue Dublin Pond, and across it, rising up above the treetops of deep red, bright yellow, and blazing orange foliage, towers Monadnock itself.

MOUNT MONADNOCK, JAFFREY-DUBLIN, NEW HAMPSHIRE. (ART DONAHUE)

"Thoreau wrote, 'That New Hampshire bluff will longest haunt our dreams.' So it had real power; people called it the 'Grand Monadnock.' Now mind you"—Mansfield chuckles—"this is before white folks in the East got out to Yosemite, Grand Canyon, or Yellowstone in any numbers."

We stand looking out and up, sharing different hiking experiences we've both had on it. It's a very doable day hike (only three to four hours round-trip), and although sections get quite rocky, it's never technical or overly tough. On summer and fall weekends and holidays, families, even those with younger children, routinely fill up the state park's lot to clamber up its popular White Dot Trail. It's often said (especially in New Hampshire) that Monadnock is second only to Japan's Mount Fuji as the most-climbed mountain in the world. Possibly. What's certain is that, long after Thoreau's inspiring 1844 climb on Monadnock, it has become a ho-hum thing to do a quick hike up and down the mountain. Indeed, most folks familiar with it try to time their hike to avoid the crowds.

"Monadnock seemed to shrink." Mansfield laughs ruefully. "It went from the 'Grand Monadnock' to being a day hike, to being sort of a granite recreational gym for a lot of people. It's still beautiful, but it has changed."

What hasn't changed, we both agree, is that Monadnock still centers the region around it, and still retains a powerful, if solitary, presence.

"In the Algonquin language it means, 'mountain that stands alone,' or 'mountain island,'" Howard says, turning to look again at the peak. "And that's really a good description for the entire Monadnock Region—it's off by itself in the southwestern corner of New Hampshire, kind of an island unto itself."

"And everything else kind of swims around it."

"Yeah, you're always moving in relation to the mountain; it's the silent hub." Howard smiles. "Whether you know it or not."

⤞⟪◆⟫⤝

On this trip to the region, I made the acquaintance of someone for whom Mount Monadnock was not merely a hub in his life. It helped save his life. Larsen Ojala grew up in nearby Rindge, New Hampshire. The mountain has always been a fixture for him.

"Any way you drive, you see it," Larsen says, tilting his black, straight-brimmed ball cap back on his wide forehead. "In Fitzwilliam, Jaffrey, Milford. And it's got such a great view on top."

Not that Ojala tends to linger long on the summit. On April 23-24, 2021, he climbed up and down Monadnock continuously for twenty-four hours, reaching the summit seventeen times. A new record.

"It was twenty-eight degrees when I started that morning," recalls Ojala, as we stand at the base of the mountain under the overhang of a picnic area, avoiding a light drizzle that's falling on a damp and overcast mid-October morning. "I believe it hovered all that night around thirty-four degrees into the next morning, when I finished."

The state of the weather aside, Ojala doesn't dwell much on the state of his stomach, which turned on him early during that twenty-four hours. He's pretty sure he could have made eighteen summits if he hadn't had to stop multiple times to vomit.

"It took me twenty-three hours and fifty-three minutes to achieve seventeen."

In reality, it took Ojala years to achieve that. And it took hitting pretty much rock bottom before he ever reached that rocky summit. At thirteen, he started abusing drugs and alcohol, eventually turning to opioids and heroin.

"I was addicted to whatever I could get my hands on, really," he says matter-of-factly, looking off into the trees nearby. He's tall, around six-three, and thin as a rail. He's got light hair and skin, true to his Scandinavian roots, with a bit of a scraggly reddish-blond goatee going on. He has a quick, toothy smile. He seems like a big, lovable, overgrown kid. But he sure made a hell out of his actual late childhood.

"I just reached a point where I couldn't keep doing it, and I didn't want to be a statistic, you know?"

"At least you got to that point," I say. "Not everyone does."

"I was so sick and tired of it. And I was willing to go to any lengths to make a better life."

At twenty-one, Ojala entered rehab.

"I couldn't make it up a set of stairs without taking a break. My legs were shot. Physically, I was a mess. I'm surprised I'm still alive, really."

Soft-spoken, humble, and self-effacing, Ojala likes to joke that his only two gifts in life were long legs and a sense of determination. As a kid, those two things carried him to whatever bad stuff he could get his hands on. Now, they were the keys to turning his still-young life around.

"I *wanted* to change. Thankfully, that was there. But also great role models and mentors and people that helped me. I mean, the mountain was basically in my backyard. I knew there were people that set records for hiking it, and I thought that was really cool. I've always been pretty good about setting goals for myself. So I made that one. And because these people helped me, I was able to achieve it."

LARSEN OJALA, MOUNT MONADNOCK. (NICK SANTOS)

Gradually, Ojala made it through rehab, got himself clean and sober, and back into good physical shape. He began training on Monadnock, then other mountains. Not hiking for mere recreation, but competitively—"power hiking," as he calls it.

"It's a high, but it's a natural high," he says. "Pushing myself mentally and physically, and it feels good. Like I'm doing something that is good and is going to benefit me, not putting some substance in my body that's gonna kill me sooner or later."

Since getting clean, Ojala also achieved some other non-hiking goals. He started his own small concrete business, got married, and has two boys now who accompany their mom and dad on hikes all over the country. He still goes to AA meetings at least once a week, and he shares his own comeback story widely with others.

"I try to give back what people have given to me."

"What do you tell people?" I wonder aloud. "What do you want people who are now where you were years ago, what do you want them to be able to get from what you've done?"

Ojala nods quietly at the question; he seems deep in thought, toes the ground a bit.

"I mean, not everyone is going to set hiking records," I continue. "Or even survive."

"I tell 'em where there's a will, there's a way," he says, hands raised. "It's the same concept with addiction, you know? I'm proof of that. You have to feel like you've had enough. But if you make that decision, and you put in the work, the results will come out of that. It's not easy. But I really believe that."

The rain has let up. We walk over to the summit trailhead.

"So, the White Dot Trail starts and ends right here," I say, patting the big wooden trail sign, still wet from the earlier rain. "This is where you had to come down and finish each lap, right? Before you headed back up."

"Yeah, right here, turn around at the sign, head back up, repeat, seventeen times. Don't even give yourself a chance to look at your truck."

"'Cause your truck was right here in the lot, right?"

"Right there," he points at a parking space, barely thirty feet away. "The exit point was right there, all day—all I had to do was get to the truck and the misery ended—I could be at home in my bed!"

No shortcuts for Larsen Ojala. There weren't any in his long and continuing recovery, and there hasn't been in his passion for hiking, either. In early May of 2023, he took to Mount Monadnock again for twenty-four hours. He summited eighteen times to set a new record, breaking his own.

The next day, I texted him my congratulations. He replied to say thanks, and invited me once again to join him on the mountain sometime. He walks faster than I run. But I did smile, thinking about this wonderful big kid I met at Monadnock, and the unlikely journey he's had. How he'd found the will to get himself free from what was killing him, and was now running free, setting records, on a mountain that stands alone.

CHAPTER 7

Green Mountains Full of
Fred & Bernie, Ben & Jerry

I take 101 West through Keene, New Hampshire, and across the Connecticut River into Vermont. The Green Mountain State. Brattleboro, minutes from both the New Hampshire and Massachusetts borders, anchors Vermont's south-eastern corner, just as Bennington does on the state's opposite (New York) side. With a population just over twelve thousand, it's a tidy, two-river (West River and the Connecticut) town, not a city.

I've always loved that it's also laced with literary threads. In the lovely public library, you'll find plenty of Archer Mayor's books. Mayor himself lives nearby in Newfane, and his "Joe Gunther" mystery series is set in Brattleboro, where Gunther is a police detective. The town also hosts a wonderful, long-running literary festival, which I have been privileged to be part of.

Hard to forget the festival's Saturday-evening get-together, held in the rolling hills of West Brattleboro at Naulakha, former home of Vermont's most famous former resident, Rudyard Kipling. (Naturally, it's located on Kipling Road, and downtown you can grab a beer at Kipling's Tavern.) In 1896, in the wake of a bitter family dispute, Kipling was forced to leave Naulakha and Vermont, never to return. He would later say to a friend, "There are only two places in the world where I want to live—Bombay and Brattleboro—and I can't live at either." Brattleboro's literary vibe has real and longtime roots.

Barely 10 miles due north of Brattleboro, along State Route 5, is Putney, Vermont. This is what your mind's eye pictures when it imagines a small Vermont town: the white clapboard Congregational church, the welcoming little diner, the white-columned historical society, and in the town center, just above little Sacketts Brook, the town's heart and soul itself, the Putney General Store. General stores are very special places because the good ones fulfill two different functions that few commercial establishments can: They sell stuff that people need, and they offer for free something people can't buy—a sense of community.

<small>PUTNEY GENERAL STORE, PUTNEY, VERMONT. (ART DONAHUE)</small>

"There are some really important resources that are critical to building a strong, vibrant community, and one of them is a general store."

Few knew more about building and maintaining strong communities than Paul Bruhn. The founder and former executive director of the Preservation Trust of Vermont, Bruhn spent forty years and most of his professional career helping people all over the state hold on to the unique and irreplaceable histories of their cities and towns. And it wasn't about some overdeveloped sense of nostalgia or sentimentality, either. It's about smart economics, like knowing that old mill complexes can be more expensive to tear down than to redevelop, and that a well-run general store can be both a community anchor *and* a competitive alternative to driving 12 miles away to the big-box store.

"The business side is really important because that's what keeps the gathering place possible," said Bruhn. "It's really not just about saving old buildings; it's about putting them to really good use."

Paul Bruhn and the Preservation Trust of Vermont pioneered a model they call community-supported enterprise, which provides an initial thrust of investment that makes it possible for a struggling entity to survive while helping the community develop the means and method of taking ownership.

When I first met Paul, he was around seventy. His health wasn't great; he walked slowly, picking his way carefully. He wasn't tall, he wasn't thin, was balding on top, but had a shock of bushy, wavy white hair all around the rest of his head. He had an elf-like face, and kind, gleaming eyes that seemed to smile along with his mouth. He had an uncommon quality of warmth and wit, patience and even grace. And in his mission of preservation, he maintained a special passion for saving

PAUL BRUHN, SHREWSBURY, VERMONT.

Vermont's general stores. What's more, with several landmark general stores that might have been lost, he found a way for the towns themselves to take control of them, and in doing so, control the fate of their futures, too.

It wasn't always easy to pull off. Money had to be raised, loans had to be granted, volunteers had to be recruited, and of those, people had to be trained to run a small, local store. He did it in Barnard, Vermont, where the lovely two-story, nearly two-hundred-year-old white-frame store across the road from pretty Silver Lake is one of the state's oldest. He did it in Shrewsbury, Vermont, where he helped to get Pierce's Store (founded 1865) reopened after it had closed for nearly a decade.

It was on the sunny front porch of Pierce's on an October afternoon in 2017 that I last talked with Paul. The store there is a great story of a community coming together and doing whatever was needed to reopen, reclaim, and renew the community resource and community gathering place that had been lost. None of those involved in the effort had any retail experience; they were local farmers, artisans, teachers, carpenters, and a cheesemaker.

"What does it say," I wonder, "that people who know nothing about running a store or a business can come together and make it work?"

"People with purpose can do anything—I've seen it!" Bruhn laughs. "But really, it shows that with a lot of passion and commitment and understanding of a really important goal, people can come together and learn entirely new skills."

PIERCE'S STORE, SHREWSBURY, VERMONT.
(ART DONAHUE)

Pierce's is run like a co-op, and while the Preservation Trust creates various ways in which it absorbs certain fixed expenses, the store ultimately must earn its keep—and survival.

"The store has to be able to provide great goods at competitive prices," Paul says with emphasis.

"It's not a charity," I add, "right?"

"It is not a charity. People need to know that they can come in here and buy a jar of pasta sauce and not pay three times what they might pay at a supermarket ten or fifteen miles away."

An older gentleman wearing a faded, light-blue, "Bernie 2016" T-shirt ambles up the porch stairs. On seeing Paul, he lights up. The two shake hands and catch up briefly before he enters the store.

"Paul, why do you think people care about general stores?" I ask. "What does America look like without a single general store?"

"It's all about community. If you don't have a gathering place like a general store or a café, there's no place for the community to come together and connect with each other. Case in point? That guy just now!" He laughs. "It's true. I remember one night we had a meeting right here, during the planning stage, and somebody who lives up the street, 'bout a hundred yards, walked in, and there was a neighbor here, and one said, 'Gee, it's great to see you—haven't seen you for about six months!' These are people who live a few hundred yards from each other. That's what a store like this provides."

Paul has to head back up to Burlington, a two-hour drive. We walk to his car; I hold his walking cane while he tosses a jacket in the backseat and prepares to get in.

"Most days, I have the best job in Vermont," he smiles. "I get to wander around and work with really amazing people, and that's the most remarkable thing about my thirty-seven years of doing this work."

"It has to feel good," I say, gesturing to the store next to us, "to have helped save places like this, community treasures."

"I mean, we like to think that we've helped, a lot, in many of these stores. But in the end, it's really the people in the community that do the heavy lifting."

He eases his way, not all that easily, into the driver's seat. I hand him the cane, which he takes and tosses in one motion in the back. I pat his arm, thank him for making the drive down to chat.

"I'd hang out here all day if I could!" he says, chuckling.

And he's off.

I wouldn't see Paul again. He died less than two years later.

In his honor, the National Park Service created the Paul Bruhn Historic Revitalization Grants Program, which helps rural communities all over America foster economic development by preserving and rehabilitating historic buildings. Across his own home state, his legacy not only endures, but continues to bring communities together, preserving some of the best and most irreplaceable things about Vermont.

-≪≪◆≫≫-

Heading a bit east from Shrewsbury brings you into Vermont's Upper Valley area. This is the Connecticut River's upper valley, which extends east into New Hampshire as well.

The Upper Valley area of Vermont includes some of its most storied towns—Barnard, Chelsea, Norwich, Pomfret, Tunbridge, Windsor, and Woodstock.

It's an area of rivers, woods, and winding roads, of farms and fields, hills and high pastureland. And in all of my travels, it's where I've met some of the most memorable people.

"Double layer of gloves here. My weak link now is my fingers—frozen 'em so many times!"

Granted, an early mid-January morning in Vermont—four inches of fresh snow overnight and still lightly falling—is not an ideal day to paint outside. Peter Huntoon has a warm and lovely studio a bit northwest of here, but that's mostly where he finishes his works.

Like a chef foraging out in the wild for the food he'll bring back indoors to prepare, Huntoon's passion is painting *en plein air*—creating outdoors in nature, with all the challenges that entails.

"After painting for thirty years, I've learned that every time I go out, it's a different scenario—the light, the weather, everything, and then something new I can't predict. So, it's a little like MacGyver, in that you have to face whatever's thrown at you on a given day and do your best to adapt."

Huntoon, a friendly, fifty-something guy with glasses who looks more like an art teacher in a ball cap and Carhartt jacket than the legendary TV action hero, nonetheless channels his own inner MacGyver. On this day, he's come to Taftsville, a village of Woodstock, to paint the iconic red covered bridge across the Ottauquechee River. But it's snowing; not helpful for mixing with wet oil paint and canvas.

PETER HUNTOON, WOODSTOCK, VERMONT

So like a real-life MacGyver, he's rigged his pickup truck with what looks like a long solar panel on the roof. He hops out of the truck, grabs a stepstool out of the back, and pulls back the panel, which forms a handy and effective small overhanging roof for him to paint under. His truck is full of little tricks he's rigged up to allow him to paint under different conditions. He shows me the wooden "box" that fits over the steering wheel, on which he can lay canvas, allowing him to paint directly from the driver's seat.

"Very clever," I have to say. "You've never done this while you're driving, right?"

"No, no."

In short order, Huntoon gets down to business. He works fast, sketches his outline, and in minutes begins applying the first daubs of paint. He's painted the bridge before, but it's been a while, and it's irrelevant now.

"I did it in the autumn before, at least fifteen years ago. Even if I painted it yesterday, today is a new day and I'm a different person."

Truth is, there are few places in his native state (born and raised in Rutland) Huntoon *hasn't* painted. He's everywhere, and he's prolific, painting hundreds and hundreds of familiar scenes and specific moments of light and life and natural beauty in the state's woods, hilltops, town centers, roads, and open fields. He's also a skilled painter with a gifted eye. But what impressed me immediately about Peter Huntoon was the passion and his outlook on life.

That snowy morning outside by the icy river was cold, raw, and physically uncomfortable. And I was well bundled up and not painting. His fingertips were cold, he was doing detailed work with his hands, occasionally standing back and jumping up and down a few times to keep the blood flowing. Sure, he knew he had only to get the basic scene roughed out here, could tidy it up in finished form back in the warm studio. But he was still there for well over an hour. You could tell his hands were cold, but his spirits were high; he laughed, he got excited when he got some detail just right, like the snow on the bridge's roof. I ambled back over to where he was working, took a peek at the canvas.

"Painting thirty years, crap weather today," I say, "but you obviously still enjoy it, still have a passion for the craft."

"Passionate, and humbled," he says, barely pausing in his work. "Because I feel like a beginner every single day. The more I learn, the more I realize there is to learn. If I know anything, it's how much I don't know. And that's wonderful because there's no end. I'll be learning passionately until the last brushstroke. What could be better?"

Huntoon reached a point where he was happy with what he'd done outside. He stepped back from his easel for an extended stretch, looking from it, to the bridge, and back. He rubbed his chin, grabbed some paper towel, and rolled his brush in it. He was done here.

"Yeah, it's a challenge, but it's such a fulfilling thing to come out, even if it's not a winner of a painting that day," he said, all the while breaking down his setup and supplies and putting things away in his truck. "It's the experience, you know? I'm addicted to coming out here and plugging myself into Mother Nature. I mean, look at this; it's beautiful here. And the longer you look, the more beauty you see."

–≪≪◆≫≫–

There are eight "Orange Counties" in America. The most famous one is in Southern California. The second-most-famous one is in Florida. The least likely one of all is in Vermont. How fitting it should also be home to the most memorable New Englander I've ever met. But then, I would have never met Fred if it hadn't been for his neighbor.

"It's very rural, still very rural, still a bunch of farms," John O'Brien says, as we sit at his kitchen table, warm inside on a bitter cold January morning in tiny Tunbridge, Vermont. With just over a thousand residents, the town sits more or less squarely in the center of the state. There's one short main street, with a general store, a town hall, public library, covered bridge, and a couple of postcard-perfect white-steepled churches. The town is nestled in the region's high, hilly pasturelands that for centuries supported dairy and sheep farming for generations of families. And every early fall since 1867, those families have streamed to the town's center for the famed Tunbridge World's Fair.

The mere mention of the Fair brings a big smile to John O'Brien's face.

"You go to the Fair, and you know, every two minutes you run into someone you went to school with or you're related to, or you do business with." He laughs. "And you're happy to see 'em—'cause it's the only time they come out of the hills!"

John's family raised sheep here. The O'Brien sheep farm abutted the Tuttle Dairy Farm, where seventh-generation Fred Tuttle was still milking his herd of Jerseys well into his seventies. True neighbors and fast friends despite being more like grandfather and grandson, John helped Fred out on the farm until he left for college, where he continued to further his passion for filmmaking.

On returning home to Tunbridge, John found Fred older, weaker, worn-out, and worn-down. John couldn't give Fred an easier job, or more money, or the dependable health care he desperately needed. But he was determined to tell the story of his lifelong friend and neighbor, a hardworking farmer fallen on hard times, too stubborn to give up, too proud to ask for help. And he did.

Shot entirely in Vermont on a shoestring budget of $100,000, with local friends and neighbors donating their time and services (and filling out the cast), *Man with a Plan* was released in 1996. The movie starred Fred Tuttle as Fred Tuttle, a broken-down Vermont dairy farmer who runs for Congress as the perfect solution to his problem: good pay, no heavy lifting, and first-class health care. (In the movie, Fred ran on a priceless campaign slogan: "I've spent my whole life in the barn; now I just want to spend a little time in the House.") In the movie, Fred wins.

The film's success was equally improbable. *Man with a Plan* became Vermont's highest-grossing independent film ever, and it made Fred Tuttle a folk hero in Vermont and, for a brief time, a bona fide celebrity, interviewed on national TV shows. Through it all, Fred was Fred—the same stooped, smiling, slightly bow-legged, imp-like, plain-speaking, overalls-wearing, "by-jee-zums"-exclaiming character he'd always been.

"Fred Tuttle is America's greatest method actor," John O'Brien was fond of saying. "I mean, he's been in character for seventy-five years."

I first met Fred and John in the heady wake of the film's release. On a blustery fall day, the three of us stood on a windy hillside in Tunbridge, Fred leaning on his cane, one hand on the visor of his blue ball cap (emblazoned with FRED) to keep it from blowing off.

I asked him what his wife, Dottie, thought of the movie.

"Hasn't seen it yet."

"No?" I asked in surprise.

"I'm sure Dottie will see it eventually, right, Fred?" John said gently.

"Why?" responded Fred with a cackle. "She says she sees enough of me already!"

I met up with Fred and John on several other occasions after that, mostly because *Man with a Plan* had an unexpected sequel. In 1998, in a move that was part political satire and part ingenious strategy to revive interest in the film, John and Fred teamed up again.

FRED TUTTLE AND JOHN O'BRIEN, TUNBRIDGE, VERMONT, 1994. (JACK ROWELL)

They took out nomination papers for Fred to run for the Republican nomination for the US Senate, which Fred promptly won.*

---

*Fred's sole opposition was a wealthy, transplanted Massachusetts businessman named Jack McMullen. The race was essentially over when, during their single debate in Burlington in October of 1998, McMullen was unable to correctly answer Fred's question, "How many teats does a cow have, Jack?" (Answer: Four.)

I promptly took off for Tunbridge to follow the state's official Republican US Senate nominee on the campaign trail for a day. At a small press gathering, Fred was asked for his thoughts on his general election opponent, incumbent Democrat, Patrick Leahy. "Oh, I like Leahy," gushed Fred. "I'm sure he's gonna win!"

And he did. And although Fred officially endorsed Leahy a week before the election, he still received more than 20 percent of the vote. Leahy, who's never lost an election, would tell me years later that the race with Fred was his closest. No matter. The two men—the former dairy farmer and the then-chairman of the powerful US Senate Judiciary Committee—became close friends. "Vermonters heard him and knew he was as authentic as they come," Leahy told me on the phone in 2012. "What you saw and heard was who he was and what you got."

In 2003, at the age of eighty-four, Fred Tuttle passed away at his home in Tunbridge. But there was yet one more unlikely chapter in the decades-long story of Fred and John's excellent adventure. Which is what brought me to Vermont and John O'Brien's farmhouse on a bright but bitter cold January morning in 2020.

"Fred still reverberates, I think, throughout Vermont culture, and certainly politics," John says, patting a big dog that's wandered into the warm kitchen and put his head on John's lap. "He still echoes. He does, he still echoes. Though, it's interesting," John says with a shrug. "A younger generation doesn't even know who he is. Just because, you know, it's twenty years ago, you have kids born and they're like, 'Who's Fred Tuttle?'"

Over those twenty years, John O'Brien continued his interest in film, ultimately completing a trilogy of films focusing on rural life in Tunbridge. He also got married, became a stepdad, and got more involved in local politics. Which wasn't entirely new for him.

"I grew up in a political family. My dad was on the state board of education and then was the state senator from Orange County. Seems like we were always protesting Nixon or nuclear power." He laughs. "My mom took little home movies and we're all holding placards in front of the state house."

Now he sits in it. In 2015, O'Brien won a seat on the Tunbridge Selectboard. Then, in 2018, he was elected to the Vermont House of Representatives.

"'Irony' doesn't even begin to describe it, does it?" I say, my hands held out. "You created a film about a Vermont farmer who runs for office and wins, and here you are twenty years later, and the filmmaker himself runs for office and wins."

"And, further irony," says John. "I was running against a dairy farmer! I used to say I'm the only filmmaker in America who can shear a sheep and milk a cow. Not sure if that's true or not."

Not surprisingly, Rep. O'Brien sits on the House Committee on Agriculture and Forestry.

As rich and remarkable as the irony of John's journey, and of this case of art-imitating-life-imitating-art, maybe it's not so implausible after all. He's a keenly intelligent, Harvard-educated man in his early sixties now. But with his tallish,

JOHN O'BRIEN FEEDING HIS SHEEP, TUNBRIDGE, VERMONT.

lean frame, wavy hair, and bright blue eyes and big smile, he projects a youthful, friendly, open vibe that feels entirely sincere and unforced. Genuine. Like Fred.

"I really like public service," John says softly, almost apologetically. "I like problem-solving. I like people."

We bundle up and head outside. It's quiet and still. The sun offers no warmth, but it does throw a bluish-gold glow on the snow-covered open field behind the house, as it stretches down the long hillside. To the west, the snowy ridges of the Green Mountains are tinged with the still-rising sun. In the near distance, a wisp of wood smoke rises straight up over a neighboring house. Next to the barn, some half-buried farm equipment peeks above the crusty snow.

We stop at the fence that pens the sheep. I ask John about the state of local dairy farming these days. He grimaces a bit, looking out at the view.

"There's only one dairy farmer left from the county who's still serving in the legislature. That's it. Used to be pretty much *all* farmers."

John's wife, Emily, comes out of the house, in her insulated coveralls, carrying a handful of carrots, which she and John feed to the few woolly sheep that've ventured up to the fence. Emily's also a photographer, and John's also a justice of the peace, both of which come in handy with the weddings that they book through the summer and fall. Wedding photos often show a happy couple posing in the field, lit up by a sunset, with curious sheep freely photobombing in the background.

WINDSOR DINER

(Windsor, VT)

THERESA RHODES, WINDSOR DINER, WINDSOR, VERMONT.

It's only fitting to have a historic diner in Windsor, a town steeped in history. Often called the "Birthplace of Vermont," the state's constitution was adopted here in 1777. Then, 175 years later, one of the last of the genuine Worcester dining cars (#835) rolled off the line and made its way north to #135 Main Street.

As you'd expect, it's snug and cozy, and from booths, to stools, to counter, adorned simply with the proven, polished details of an irreplaceable original. It's also the only diner I've ever visited that is owned and run as an almost entirely solo operation.

I watched in wonder as Theresa Rhodes took an order at the counter, made a new pot of coffee, finished up an order of bacon and eggs on the grill, and in one motion turned and slid the plate under the raised eyebrows of a customer who's been watching with the same sense of seeing something unusual.

"Your comfort food, my dear!" Rhodes says with a flourish, pivoting back to the grill.

"How do you do this all by yourself?" I ask.

"Motivation," she says brightly. "I think of it like a puzzle, or each day as a project, and every day is different. And I have help on weekends!"

On this day, Rhodes—a smallish, sprightly, forty-something mom—had the added project of making sure that twenty-five hot meals were getting prepared in the basement; it's her commitment to help locals who are food-insecure.

"We don't have a pantry or soup kitchen in town," she says, tearing off some plastic wrap and handing it to a volunteer. "We got a grant, so that helps, but it's important, you know, especially during the colder season, to have a hot meal and some emotional support."

That sense of community, it strikes me, is what diners are really all about. It also strikes me, while we're chatting in the basement, that there's no staff at all upstairs.

"Ha!" Rhodes laughs. "During COVID, I did a year-plus with no help. I'd run down here, make some bread, some pies, and I'd leave a pager on the counter with a little sign to page me if someone came in. It worked fine!"

Only in Vermont. Only at a special diner run by one of the most marvelously multitasking diner owners I've ever met.

"It's very hard to make a living on a farm anymore," says John. "We can make a lot more using the beauty of the farm as a venue than we can selling wool."

Emily heads back into the house. John has to make the forty-minute drive north to the state house in Montpelier. We stand by the house for a moment, our breath coming out in big puffs of vapor.

"I can point you to Fred's gravesite if you want to go by."

"You must miss him," I say.

"Yeah." He nods. "It seems like on a day like today, with you here, it seems like, wait, I must be going down to Fred's, picking him up, and we're off on some adventure with him." John idly wipes away some loose snow from the hood of his car. "He would love to go to the state house; he'd just sit out in the lobby and talk to people all day long."

Then John is off, his car crunching on the packed snow, slowly descending down the hilly road between the bare trees.

I felt glad to have visited. It felt like finishing a favorite book, having learned the last chapter of the John O'Brien and Fred Tuttle story. By jeezums, that was a good friendship.

-·≺≺≺◆≫≫≫·-

Along with maple syrup, leafy falls, and lefty politics, Vermont also defines skiing in New England. It may well be where modern skiing in America began.

In 1934, the first ski lift—a rope tow powered by a Model-T car engine—carried skiers up a hill on Clinton Gilbert's farm in Woodstock. Two years later, on another hillside farm in East Corinth, another rope tow began service. Decades later, the only thing that's gone up since then at Gilbert's Hill is a state historical marker. In East Corinth, meanwhile, the venerable rope tow has become the oldest continuously operating ski lift in North America.

WADE PIERSON, DODGE DART, EAST CORINTH, VERMONT.
(ABAGAEL GILES / VERMONT PUBLIC)

And it's still powered by a 1973 Dodge Dart with a Slant-Six engine, sitting in a slope-side wooden shed.

"It's definitely not what somebody is expecting if they're thinking 'ski resort.'" Wade Pierson chuckles. "We're definitely not a resort. We're a *ski* area. On a great old hill that's just a gem of outdoor, natural Vermont beauty."

All true. Especially the "not a resort" part.

Wade Pierson knows the hill as well as anyone. Local kid, he grew up skiing on the hill. He still lives and works nearby, and today is volunteer manager of Northeast Slopes, the beloved little ski hill on VT Route 25, just northwest of the East Corinth General Store. He's hardly the only volunteer; there's no paid staff. Northeast Slopes is a rarity the likes of which one can count on one warm, mittened hand: an entirely volunteer, community-owned, and community-run ski area.

"For one thing," says Pierson as we stand at the base of the hill on a brisk but clear January afternoon, "it's not only physically accessible, but it's financially accessible to anybody and everybody, and we take extra efforts to make that happen, especially for the surrounding communities."

Truth is, despite the influx of upscale newcomers over the recent past, more than 10 percent of Vermonters live below the poverty line, and there are real pockets of that in and around East Corinth. Skiing, needless to say, is not an inexpensive sport. I've been lucky enough to ski since I was a kid, and I love the sport itself. I've come to despise, however, the overall industry. A full complement of new ski equipment can easily cost up to $2,000 or more. For a family of four, a single day on the slopes at a major ski resort can cost over $600. Lessons, rentals? Hundreds of dollars more.

NORTHEAST SLOPES, EAST CORINTH, VERMONT. (BRIAN CARROLL)

Northeast Slopes? I paid twelve bucks for a half-day ticket. That'll *maybe* buy you a soft drink at Aspen. The sad reality is that the ski industry has utterly priced out a vast portion of the population from ever taking up skiing. And it sucks.

"Look over your shoulder," says Pierson.

I glance over at the little T-bar loading area, where kids are whooping and laughing as they ready to ride up the hill.

"That's what I love most. There are fifty-five kids here this afternoon from the local school, and for most of 'em, this is probably not something they've experienced on their own or would be able to in today's ski industry."

The schoolkids ski for free. No equipment? No problem. Ski equipment is donated to the "Ski Library," which outfits kids with whatever they need. Free. The woman driving the actual school bus bringing the kids here hops off as they get ready, and runs the beginner rope tow lifts herself. The hill's been groomed overnight by a veteran Vermont ski groomer who, on his two nights off working at bigger mountains, runs over to East Corinth and grooms the hill. The ski lodge is still the original little red wooden building no bigger than a two-car garage, filled with a bunch of old, beaten-up picnic tables.

"We talked about changing the lodge," says Pierson, scratching his head. "But we thought we'd lose that traditional feel, the coziness, you know? Besides, we can't afford it!"

A little kitchen counter at one end of the lodge has a fridge and a propane stove, and serves up the hill's signature "Nor'easter burger," served on a toasted Kaiser roll with pickles and fries. It was delicious. Six bucks. I'd try to estimate what six bucks would buy you at Breckenridge, but already know it won't buy you a damned thing.

I strike up a chat with a teacher who's helping chaperone the kids; she's retiring soon, and points out to me how many adult volunteers—working the grill, the lifts, driving buses—are former students of hers.

"You know, in a town like ours, we actually have a very high poverty rate. Sad but true. And for a lot of these kids, this is the only opportunity they'd ever have to ski."

"That's a thing to be thankful for," I say.

"Thank Wade! He organized all this for the kids!"

For his part, Wade's pretty ho-hum and humble about it all.

"We've got a few generations now of folks who grew up here, or nearby, and who are bringing their kids, their grandkids, here to ski. And many of them volunteer in some way. It's great, keeps it going."

"You know how rare this is," I say, before getting my own ski boots on.

"There used to be many, many more community ski hills in Vermont," says Wade. "Now we're down to four or five, some of them private. Long as people'll keep supporting us, we'll keep it going."

Wade gestures to a bin beside the rope tow; it's full of big work gloves to borrow for the ride up. That rope is rough, and it yanks a bit. Been a while since I rode one. This relic is super-fast and in a shot I'm off, and up the hill. The ride down is a surprise. Short, for sure, but more of a pitch than I expected. And no lift line going back up.

"Not bad, huh?" says Wade at the bottom, laughing.

"Not bad at all, sir!"

Before leaving, I ask him if I can see the famous Dodge Dart. We walk over to a ramshackle wooden shed at the base of the beginner rope tow.

"Voila!" says Wade, spreading his arms and beaming like a proud parent. "Forty years, and still purring like a kitten, still getting those kids up the hill!"

⸻

From East Corinth, it's about 10 miles down VT 25 to Bradford and Interstate 89, then a half-hour to White River Junction, and off onto pretty VT 4, and the winding, fifteen-minute drive to Woodstock, which may, or may not, be the state's most picture-perfect postcard town. (All the tourist brochures say so.)

Granted, on a winter night, with snow falling and lights twinkling, its town green looks like the real-life Bedford Falls. There's certainly a lot of money here. (Like the Rockefeller-owned Woodstock Inn.) Alas, the money doesn't extend to the struggling little business I was stopping by at. It might be doing better if, like the market across the street, it sold some of modern Vermont's signature products—artisanal cheese, craft beer, organic salsa, homemade hot chocolate mixes that sell for $20 per (cute-as-a-button) box. Instead, it sells a product whose value has never decreased, even as its status has been reduced to relic: a local newspaper.

"All right, let's talk," says Phil Camp, zipping up his parka and clapping his big, downy mittens together. "I promise not to wave to my fan club if they drive by!"

We're standing on Elm Street in Woodstock, just off the town center, and just outside the sturdy, white, three-story wooden building that's home to the *Vermont Standard*, the state's oldest (founded 1853) continuously published weekly newspaper.

"We're in business to give people what they want, what they need, and what they deserve as citizens. How's that? Simple enough?"

Before I can respond, the first honk/wave chimes in. No surprise.

Phil Camp, wiry, white-haired, and spirited at ninety, is among the area's most beloved residents. He grew up here, worked at the paper as a teen, went off to college, made a good living helping shepherd the growth of Killington Ski Resort, and in 1981 saved the failing *Standard* by buying it.

"I may be its president, but it's not my newspaper. It's the community's newspaper. I bought it to pay this town back for what they did for me," says Camp softly, his voice catching. "They raised me. They raised me."

The paper's been through it all, and then some. An 1867 fire destroyed its original building. A flood in 1973 destroyed its

PHIL CAMP, WOODSTOCK, VERMONT. (BOB OLIVER)

presses. In the wake of Tropical Storm Irene in 2011, the paper's offices were flooded out and ruined. In 2018, another fire destroyed its new building. Camp is nothing if not a determined, forward-thinking optimist. And the most stubborn of Yankees.

"We publish! That's what we do," says Camp, arms outstretched. "The community expects it, and we respect our responsibility in that."

The sad truth is, with local print publications, that expectation has steadily declined. Everywhere. Decade by decade, disinterest and digital devices are inexorably destroying what floods and fires couldn't. What's come to be called the "local news desert"—entire municipalities, whole regions no longer served by a credible news platform with local reporting—is lapping at the edges of Woodstock and all of the ten towns in Vermont's Upper Valley. The *Standard* is in trouble.

"In just the last decade, two thousand newspapers have gone down. Gone. Sixty-five percent of them are local weeklies. Just like us."

Not that they're giving up on Elm Street. The pared-down staff of a dozen or so, led by publisher Dan Cotter, forges ahead, focusing on local news and issues that matter here.

In a lively morning story meeting, Cotter and editor Tess Hunter trade some ideas. Phil Camp, in person after a recent illness, studiously scribbles some notes.

"That commitment to getting out the local news, that's Phil's passion," says Hunter during a break. "He is so passionate about his paper, and we all want to support him in that. This is a town that has had a nonstop paper and a steady stream of local news for 160-plus years." In a hint of fatalism that eludes her boss, she adds, "They will notice when it's gone."

What is, in fact, lost when local news platforms shutter and close, leaving a dried-up information landscape where once it was tracked and reported on for the public good?

"We are the quintessential old-style hometown weekly newspaper, that's covering everything from the select board and the economic development commission meetings to the local historical society meetings at the grange hall in a small town in Vermont," says senior staff writer Tom Ayres.

Ayres, a bespectacled sixty-something, is a quasi-retired, former elected public official from Burlington, Vermont. He knows well what it means to be in the weeds of public process and governance. It ain't sexy, but it sure can be significant. Small details that may arise at say, a planning or financial commission meeting, far from public view, but that impact local lives nonetheless. Traditionally, journalists have been the public's eyes and ears as the local government process unfolds. Except in more and more towns and cities, many of these meetings unfold in the dark, with fewer, or no, journalists.

"You're at these meetings, big and small," I say to Ayres. "That means there's at least a basic level of accountability—reporters present to record what's said, what's done—that otherwise is just plain missing, right?"

"Absolutely. But it's more," says Ayres. "So we tie what's happening in a town like Woodstock or Bridgewater around housing issues, around child care, and we're able to write about those on a very local level, but we're also able to tie it into a state and national context. I mean, that's what all local newspapers did, but so many of them are gone now. Where they're gone, much of it is just filtered through social media."

"Hardly the same."

"Right, not at all the same," agrees Ayres. "People who pick up the *Standard* every week know these stories are being reported through the lens of someone who's following it every week, keeping them abreast of what's going on. A reporter who's in those meetings."

"Until there is no reporter in those meetings."

"Well, yeah," says Ayres, throwing his hands up. "We hope to avoid that here."

So does Phil Camp.

"It's real simple," he says. "You lose your local newspaper, the thing that ties everything in town, everything in the area together, and you lose track of each other. They lose their voice, they don't have any input, for community life. You just wander around like strangers."

But Camp is also a realist. At his age, he has to be. He knows it's going to take someone like him—a person with both deep pockets and a deep sense of civic good—to come in and do what he did decades ago: save the local newspaper. It may happen. It may not. Many are the Woodstocks across America, towns that long supported a great local paper until the support dried up, and the town was overtaken instead by the insidious, deadening creep of the local news desert. Still, Camp's bedrock belief in the basic good sense of his town, his state, is tough to shake.

"Vermonters look out for each other. We tend to do the right thing," says Camp, looking down the street, seeming to nod unconsciously. "These people understand how lucky they are to have a newspaper like the *Vermont Standard*."

Phil darts back inside the office, wants to make sure I have some copies of the paper's current issue to take with me. I stand there, thinking that a big part of my stopping by was not simply to see how things stood with the paper, but almost more as a silent thank-you for the fact they were still hanging on at all, still fighting the good fight. I hated the feeling that it was like paying respect to the dying.

Camp was back with an armload of papers. We shook hands. I wished him well, but it still felt more like elegy than encouragement.

"Hang in, Phil. Keep up the good work here."

"Oh, we will." He smiled, gripping my hand with one arm while tucking the papers securely under my elbow with the other. "We will!"

West on Route 4, a few miles from Woodstock, brings you out to Route 100, easily the greenest of the roadways running through the Green Mountain National Forest. In summer and early fall, driving through the steep, densely wooded narrowness of Brandon Gap, past the plunging water of Granville's Moss Glen Falls, you can feel the mist through an open car window. Just past the falls lie the towns of Warren, and 10 miles further, Waitsfield. Both storied ski towns, both as Vermont as it gets.

On a trip in the fall of 2018, it wasn't ski trails, the beer trail, the cheese trail, or any other Vermont-inspired (and modern-marketer-driven) trail I was after. It was tree houses. They seemed to be sprouting all over the state; many were complex, creative, and even luxurious enough to be offered as unusual outdoor "rooms" at some upscale Vermont inns. My interest, however, was focused on one single person who had become something of a tree-house legend and pioneer, and whose small company in Warren had built dozens of truly unique tree houses. But I knew my first question would be about his name, and where "B'fer" came from.

"My dad would come home every day and say, 'Hello, James B-for-Burton Roth!' I thought I had two middle names, and I kinda liked 'B-fer,' so it stuck!"

"And you must have had a tree house."

"Believe it or not, I never had a tree house as a little kid," says James Burton Roth. "I built a tree house for myself right after I got out of college. I was twenty-four, and for five years, I lived in it every summer into fall until the first snow would fly in Vermont. I even had my first date with my wife in the tree house."

"That's different."

"I'm pretty sure that's what won her over thirty years ago!"

Roth may not have had a tree house as a kid, but it's safe to say he's been more than making up for that ever since. For one thing, even at a youthful sixty, he's surprisingly childlike, standing about five-foot-ten, slim and agile, with a long shock of gray hair pulled back and flowing over his collar. He laughs quickly, easily, often. If he's not laughing, he's smiling. Broadly. One gets the sense that this is a happy man.

"What is it, in general, about tree houses?" I ask. "There's a kind of magic, right?"

"There's something about being in a tree house that just hits you at your whole core essence of being a kid," says Roth, smiling and nodding. "It's the childhood experience of being up in the tree and escaping the reality of real homes and school and all that. It's just a way to get up and away from all that. There's a fairy-tale notion."

"I had that, too," I say. "Right in the backyard, couple of two-by-fours, nothing fancy. But what accounts for the whole new popularity, with adults?"

"There's this escapism involved, there's getting back to nature," Roth says, looking about the woods near where we're standing. "A lot of what you see nowadays, people are intrigued by a tree house and they want to get closer to nature. I personally think it's more that they want to get closer to their inner kid. As for myself, as a sixty-year-old kid, I've got an occupation that keeps me from having to grow up!"

JAMES "B'FER" ROTH. (DANA JINKINS)

Roth did start out as a striving young adult. He grew up in Michigan, left Michigan State after two years, hitchhiked around the country, ended up in Warren, Vermont. He got a degree from Johnson State College, built that first tree house here, got married, and set about with a partner being a rustic furniture maker and home builder. In 2000, the furniture makers were approached by the Make-A-Wish Foundation, in conjunction with a design-build school in Warren, to construct a tree house for kids with disabilities.

"That was our first real professional job, all volunteer labor and donated materials," says Roth, smiling at the memory. "I'll tell you, to get a kid in a wheelchair up into a tree house, under his or her own power, well, it's just a magnificent thing. That was it. We were hooked."

More tree house jobs came in, including one for Paul Newman's Hole in the Wall Gang Camp. By 2005, Roth and his partner were focusing entirely on tree houses, and have been ever since.

"We've built our tree houses now in twenty-five states, or halfway across the country. Halfway to our goal of building one in every state!"

A typical tree house can take four or five weeks to build; a wheelchair-accessible one can take three months or more to finish. It's clear that Roth loves everything about what he does. It's equally clear that the feeling is mutual.

"I describe it like Dr. Seuss in Vermont for kids," says Catherine Benham. "It's hard to describe until you see it because it's just fun. Everybody who shows up is always amazed at how whimsical it is and how spectacular."

She's right. We greet her at the front door of her Warren, Vermont, home, walk through the kitchen, where she opens the back door, and . . . there is a suspension walkway straight out to a huge tree, where indeed, something exactly out of Dr. Seuss beckons. The roof tilts off at different angles; windows, too.

"The one thing that's square is the floor!" says Benham, laughing. "Yeah, it's pretty incredible."

The tree house is more than incredible. It's also a memorial. In July, 2008, Benham's husband was diagnosed with pancreatic cancer. He wanted to leave his two children, then ten and twelve, something to remember him by.

MICHAEL'S TREE HOUSE, WARREN, VERMONT. (DANA JINKINS)

"He called me," B'fer Roth recalls. "He said he was dying. He had this idea of raising this gazebo they had in the yard, up and onto a tree he'd cut. He asked me if I could help him do that. I didn't know Michael that well then. And I'm taking this in. I told him, Michael, we can do better than that. We will do far better than that. I saw it immediately as a community effort, 'cause that's the kind of community it is. And that's what it became."

Roth designed the tree house, orchestrated the building, and set about with a large group of people to build immediately. They knew Michael's severe prognosis; it was months, maybe.

"And they came here, and we got to watch it," says Benham. "Michael got to watch it. He was so weak he couldn't participate the way he would want to. But he, we and the kids, helped put the roof on. B'fer saw to that. It was a very dark time in our lives. But this was joy and fun and memories and community support."

Late that fall, soon after the tree house was completed, Michael Benham died.

"And your husband left this legacy," I say. "Which is what he wanted."

"He did," Benham nods slightly. "And he gets remembered every time anybody looks at this."

"I mean, we were all bawling when we were done," says Roth. "And to know that, that would be something his kids would remember him by, it was truly special." There's silence, a wind in the high branches. "People sometimes ask me if I have a favorite tree house. It's Michael. Michael's tree house."

The work continues. Roth has grandkids now. The hair's still long, the smile still ever-present. These days, he's most proud of his work on accessibility, and particularly of a design technique he helped engineer that allows wheelchair ramps to curve directly up and into a tree house.

"To me, those are my favorite projects, that get kids in chairs up into trees. Getting into a tree is such a basic childlike experience, and if you're left out of that with a disability, yeah, that's a bummer. You watch a kid in a chair, you say, go for it, you got it. And they do. And you see that smile light up at the end of that ramp ride . . . wow. There is nothing more satisfying to me than that. Period."

COUNTRY GIRL DINER

(Chester, VT)

COUNTRY GIRL DINER, CHESTER, VERMONT. (JENNIFER URE-PLATT)

Hands down, my favorite *kind* of diner: longtime, authentic classic that was closed, saved, and reopened. But the Country Girl Diner has an extra, wonderful twist on that. Its owners, Jess Holmes and her husband, Paul Frasca, had long harbored a dream of owning a diner. How long? For Holmes, it goes back to childhood.

"In my teens, I did a paper, was asked what magazine you'd want to be in and what would the article be about. I wrote that I always wanted a diner, that it would be *Yankee* magazine, and it would be of the ten-best diners in America. It's a dream come true for both of us!"

Frasca smiles, nods to me in agreement. "She has to kind of remind me we own the place. Like, really—we *own* it."

The diner itself, a genuine Silk City dining car (serial #178), was built in Paterson, New Jersey, in 1944. It served first in Jaffrey, New Hampshire; it's been in its present location since 1966. It was closed for years before the revitalization began in 2011. Frasca and Holmes, both veterans of the food biz (he'd been chef for the previous owner), leapt at the chance to keep the diner going, and bought it in 2017.

It's sleek, shiny, warm, and cozy; it says "home," which is how it should be. The couple were even married at the diner.

"It's our town, our home; it's family," says Frasca. "It's like I'm cooking breakfast at home—but there's two hundred people coming over!"

"This is a huge part of the community," says Holmes. "Everybody gathers here."

Including the Q-Tip Girls. I knew that because that's what the back of their blue T-shirts read, which I couldn't miss as I walked by the counter—along with the three big, bright, white hairdos.

"One guess!" One of the women laughed when I asked about the name.

"Umm, don't tell me," I hesitated, hands up. "The white hair?"

"Yes! A friend would come in here and say, 'Hi, Q-Tip one, hi, Q-Tip two, hi, Q-Tip three.'"

"So, is this the official diner of the Q-Tips?"

"Absolutely!"

It's also officially one of the best Vermont breakfasts I've ever had. Big omelet, thick-cut, cured bacon, with lots of sharp Vermont cheddar. From flour, cheese, farm-fresh eggs, and maple syrup, it's all locally sourced. To watch the owners work, bouncing from grill to booths and back again, quick waves and greetings to regulars, is to watch two people doing exactly what they love. In 2023, in its March/April edition, *Yankee* magazine featured the Country Girl Diner. A teenager's decades-old dream has come true.

CHAPTER 8

A West Side Story: The Berkshires

Vermont Route 7 hugs the western part of the state as it heads south, threading through the southern part of the Green Mountain National Forest, passing through Danby, Dorset, Manchester, Bennington, before finally plunging across the Massachusetts border at Williamstown. Thirty-five miles further south is Stockbridge, the gravitational center of the Berkshires. Between western Massachusetts and the state's far more populous and politically powerful eastern side, there's long been a divide that feels far wider than the actual 130 miles. With justification, the western part of the state often feels slighted and ignored. (Not, however, by waves of summering New Yorkers.) In truth, the soft, rolling hills of the Berkshires are a beautiful and blessed counterweight to the rough-and-tumble of the coast's port cities and sprawling suburban development. Culturally, the Berkshires are still the state's freethinking frontier, and have long drawn artists, those seeking a new start, or just a place to get away.

"Hey, if I can move to the Berkshires, anyone can!"

So joked former New York Yankees pitcher Jim Bouton on a crisp fall day back in 2008.

Bouton, author of the groundbreaking and highly controversial book, *Ball Four,* had retired from baseball in 1978, and moved to the tiny Berkshires town of South Egremont. As he tossed tennis balls to his dog on a long, sloping hill behind his house, he joked that no one believed that he was now a Red Sox fan.

I pointed out that he was wearing a Yankees hat.

MONUMENT MOUNTAIN, GREAT BARRINGTON, MASSACHUSETTS. (ART DONAHUE)

"Oh, that," he laughed.

Later, his wife told me she'd only asked him to remove it once.

"It was hunting season," she said. "I told him, Honey, the woods out there are full of Red Sox fans. And they have guns."

James Weldon Johnson came here to get away, too. Like Bouton, he was also from New York. Unlike Bouton, he had a career that had included pretty much everything *except* baseball. Born in 1871 to Bahamian immigrants, Johnson was a gifted writer and poet, and became a celebrated voice of the famed Harlem Renaissance period. A lawyer by training, he was a diplomat for President Theodore Roosevelt, serving as consul to both Venezuela and Nicaragua. An ardent civil rights activist, he was the first Black executive secretary of the NAACP, and the first Black professor hired by New York University. In collaboration with his brother, musical composer John Rosamond Johnson, Johnson also composed the lyrics for "Lift Ev'ry Voice and Sing," often referred to as the "Negro National Anthem."

PIONEER VALLEY, MASSACHUSETTS, LOOKING WEST TO THE BERKSHIRES. (ART DONAHUE)

Given Johnson's prolific and far-flung life of diverse pursuits, it's perhaps not surprising that, by 1926, his doctor advised him to relax a bit more for his health. With his wife, civil rights activist Grace Nail Johnson, the couple found a lovely barn in Great Barrington, Massachusetts. They renovated it, and "Five Acres," as they dubbed it, became the Johnsons' home and haven away from the stress and bustle of New York. In the woods behind the house, just across a small brook, they built a one-room cabin. There, Johnson would write for entire days, producing some of his signature works, including his 1934 autobiography, *Along This Way*, as well as *God's Trombones*, a book of verse. Tragically, Johnson was killed in an auto accident in 1938 in Wiscasset, Maine. His wife, Grace, survived, and lived to the age of ninety-one.

Fast-forward some seventy years.

It's 2011, and another Black couple is looking for a getaway place in the Berkshires. But not just any place. They've learned that the former home of James Weldon Johnson is for sale. What makes it more astonishing than merely coincidental is that only a year earlier, Jill Rosenberg Jones was named executor of the James Weldon Johnson literary estate. A year later, on a cold January day with several feet of snow on the ground, Jill and her husband, Rufus Jones, and their young son Jacob, were being shown the house by a local realtor.

JAMES WELDON JOHNSON, WRITING CABIN AT "FIVE ACRES," GREAT BARRINGTON, MASSACHUSETTS. (BEINECKE RARE BOOK AND MANUSCRIPT LIBRARY, YALE UNIVERSITY)

"We drove up from Jersey City," recalls Rufus. "There were four-foot snow-banks around the house, icicles hanging off the roof, most of it was covered in snow, and it was definitely not the time to show a house."

And yet, Jill and Rufus, both financial industry professionals, found themselves entranced by the rustic little remodeled barn, whose history seemed to still be in the air.

"When I walked into the home, there was no furniture, and there were two rays of sun coming straight down from the tall windows and the cathedral ceiling," says Rufus. "And I felt embraced. I felt like we belonged here and this was going to be our place."

And so it has been. With some minor modernizations, the home has been kept largely the same as it was when Johnson owned it. On a late summer day in 2021, I'm standing in the airy living room with Rufus, looking up at the cathedral ceiling.

"So, Rufus, this is the original interior of the barn?"

"It is, and we have photographs of Grace and Johnson sitting right here in their chairs."

"Most of the timber looks original."

"It's all the original hand-hewn beams," says Rufus, pointing up. "The hayloft up there, everything you see is the way it was in 1927, when they refurbished the barn into living quarters."

But embracing James Weldon Johnson's former home now seems merely a metaphor for how Jill and Rufus Jones have embraced his entire legacy, intent on sharing it, and educating more people about it.

"Johnson was an extraordinary American," says Jill. "He is under-recognized in terms of what he did for the country, and for the world."

Then came the discovery in the woods.

Jill and Rufus Jones knew about Johnson's writing cabin; they had seen a photograph of Johnson himself posing in front of it. But locals insisted that the writing cabin, if it had existed, must have long since been lost to decades of neglect, reclaimed by the weather, wild brush, and overgrown woods. When the realtor pointed out to the woods where he thought the cabin may have been, the couple tracked across four feet of snow in the falling light. And found it.

Now, retracing their steps from that winter dusk, Jill and Rufus lead me across a meadow in the warm sunshine, off onto a short, wooded path, opening to a small, shaded clearing just above the brook. And there's the cabin.

"Surprise," I say.

"Surprise," smiles Rufus, spreading his arms. "In 2010, when we discovered that this house and property were here, the word around town was that this cabin did not exist."

It does exist. But barely.

"Watch your step," says, Rufus, opening the cabin door, and allowing me a peek inside.

The contours of a rustic, one-room writing cabin are clearly visible, including a built-in platform to accommodate a mattress, allowing Johnson to take a nap during a writing break. But the wood is rotting and disintegrating; parts of the floor sag and cannot be stepped on. The roof is the bigger concern; a giant tarp covers it now. But Jill and Rufus see something more than a still-standing-but-rotting relic in the woods.

"The vision is to restore it," says Jill, with a sweep of her hand, as we stand again outside the cabin in the filtered, leafy, late-afternoon sunlight. "Restore it to almost exactly as it was when Johnson had it. Even with modern protective elements that will help preserve it further, we want it to look exactly as it did when Johnson was writing here."

JILL AND RUFUS JONES, WRITING CABIN, "FIVE ACRES," GREAT BARRINGTON, MASSACHUSETTS.

In 2016, Jill and Rufus Jones formally created the James Weldon Johnson Foundation, a nonprofit whose mission is to advance the legacy of Johnson through research, educational programs, and artistic residencies in partnership with neighboring Bard College at Simon's Rock.

"They are intent on supporting artists who are going to illuminate Johnson's story through visual arts," says Meclina Priestley, who had come out to be with Jill and Rufus on the day we visited. In 2017, Priestley, a talented artist who creates portraits using micro-calligraphy, was among the first five residency artists selected. "I think Jill and Rufus are looking at the cabin partly as a metaphor," says Priestley. "But also as a physical space where writers, researchers, students can go and learn."

And they have been.

"I do think there is something about that space that's kind of amazing," says John Weinstein, provost of Bard College at Simon's Rock. "It's one of the many reasons I love bringing student groups there. To connect them in a real, physical way with James Weldon Johnson, who is this largely unknown but leading player in major roles, the first to do things in so many areas. And we'll go and look in the cabin, and then we'll sit in a circle and read a passage from *God's Trombones*, written right there in the cabin."

The cabin—symbol, center, historic site—along with the foundation itself, has received significant fund-raising support, and is now in the midst of a full renovation and preservation project. But that broad and growing support was still in the future during my visit in 2021.

After visiting the cabin in the woods, we walked back over the brook, through the field, and returned to the house at Five Acres. It was still hot, even late in the day. There was still an unmistakable joy that Jill and Rufus seemed to exude in sharing their story, their hopes, their plans. Even talking to each other, they beamed when pointing and gesturing around the property, imagining changes and visions yet to happen. And in all of it, they continually stressed how unlikely it all was, and their sense that James Weldon Johnson seemed to have found *them*, not the reverse.

"Do you feel," I wonder as we stand on the cool lawn beside the house, "that in addition to being the residents of Johnson's home, you're really now the stewards of his legacy, too?"

"It is an incredible responsibility, but one that fills us with love," says Jill. "Yes, we are the stewards."

So they are. Working away at their day jobs, taking care of family, all at the same time while passionately engaged in preserving the legacy of a remarkable American we all should know more about.

"We'll just keep making friends and relationships and enjoying this labor of love with others," says Rufus, as we shake hands. "It's a beautiful thing, you know. It's a blessing to be here, and a blessing to have this responsibility."

—⦉⦉◆⦊⦊—

CHAPTER 9

Into New England's "Deep South"

There are six New England states. But all of them evolved differently. Both Vermont and Maine were initially territories. After Massachusetts, the colonies in Connecticut and Rhode Island took shape next, both in 1636. Which is ironic. Connecticut, as the southernmost New England state, has inevitably been influenced by New York's powerful gravitational pull. (So have the Berkshires and southern Vermont.) Northeastern Connecticut, especially its lovely "Quiet Corner," with towns like Putnam, Woodstock, and Brooklyn, looks and feels quintessentially New England.

Then there's the Interstate 95 corridor as it hugs Long Island Sound for most of the 90 miles between New London and Stamford. These are the big coastal cities of Connecticut—New Haven, Bridgeport, Norwalk. By the time you reach Stamford and Greenwich, you're less than 10 miles from White Plains, New York, and only an hour from Midtown Manhattan. Here, in southwestern Connecticut, there's only a slender, tendril-like connection to New England. New York Yankees fans comprise a majority of five of Stamford's six zip codes; the sixth splits fifty-fifty—between Yankees and *Mets* fans.

In the summer of 2022, after many forays over the years through the state's northern, middle, and coastal areas (including Stamford), I decided to look for a part of southern Connecticut that, while close to New York, seemed more of New England. Woodbury, at the southern edge of Litchfield County, is less than 30 miles from the New York border. With its smooth, sculpted hills, farms, and pretty, small town centers, it looks and feels like parts of New Hampshire, Vermont, or the Berkshires.

Not that New York's close proximity has no effect.

"I lived in Chelsea in Manhattan for three and a half years, on and off. And the food here is better, much better," says Edward Tufte. "And it's very calm, like a wonderful dream."

Tufte is among the most peculiar people I've met in my travels. A renowned statistician, author, and professor in the field of data visualization, he's also an artist, passionate about pushing the envelope in design and sculpture. Big sculpture. Rusted old bulldozers, bridge beams, railroad tracks. Stuff that needs a lot of space.

He found that in southwestern Connecticut.

"There are seven small ridges here where the glaciers went through," Tufte tells me, standing on the summer grass, squinting back up through the sun at the top of a ridge. "It feels like a getaway here, isolated from the rest of the world. So serene and quiet, which I emphasize in my sculpture, and it just works so well for this."

Edward Tufte, often referred to as "ET," retired from teaching in 1999. Nearing eighty when we met, he's a lean, slight man, with thinning but wavy grayish-blond hair, wire-rimmed glasses, and a restless, sort of fidgety energy. In 2005, he bought 234-acre Woodbury Farm, renaming it Hogpen Hill Farms. Today, with its rolling ridges, sloping hills, and wide-open fields all dotted with areas of woods, the farm is a sweeping, outdoor canvas on which to manipulate an ever-evolving sculpture park. It's open to the public, and the land will remain permanently open and undeveloped. There are one hundred of Tufte's pieces scattered over the landscape here, some more abstract than others. All of them, Tufte suggests, require some thought, some ruminating. He's not interested in people walking briskly by, like in a museum.

"I used to have a sign coming up the driveway, a diamond-shaped sign. It said, 'Shut up and look.' Because it's all about *seeing* here, it's not about words."

Another sign here reads, "If you see something, say nothing."

"I love when I see people walking around a piece, looking at it from all sides," says Tufte, smiling. "They won't say a word to each other. And it might go on for ten minutes, in total silence."

"You want people to just look, just *be* here."

"Exactly. And the reaction is so wonderful. Honestly, from schoolchildren to art historians, a total escape; not thinking about all the other stuff going on, just being in the moment."

I will say, standing directly underneath an authentic, full-size aluminum-silver, vintage Airstream trailer, suspended in the air and outfitted with rocket boosters as if about to be launched into space, does tend to focus the mind in the moment.

"The thing about sculptures," Tufte says animatedly, raising both hands, "is that they're always different. Every day that I come out, it's different—I'm at a different distance, it's raining, the dog is running around it—it's a fresh experience. When I have a painting on the wall, after a month, I can't see it anymore. I have to move it."

In truth, sometimes he feels the same way about his sculptures. Even the really big ones.

"We've moved the Airstream rocket, which is very difficult. It's eighty feet long."

AIRBORNE AIRSTREAM TRAILER, WOODBURY, CONNECTICUT. (BOB OLIVER)

"Something just seemed off to you?"

"I'm picky. If I don't like it, we move it. We've moved that three times. Couple of backhoes. Once we moved it about eighteen inches."

That is picky.

We'd been sitting and chatting for nearly half an hour, and Tufte seemed impatient to get on with his day, which I encouraged him to do.

"That's fine," he said, jumping up, "but first I have to show you the Bamboozler."

We walked over to possibly the tallest grove of waving bamboo I've ever seen, some stalks easily between fifteen and twenty feet high. And it was a maze; paths had been cut between the dense bamboo. I followed him up one path, down another, around a corner, to a small sitting area with two plastic chairs. It was lushly green, shaded entirely from the bright sun. But most of all, it was remarkably quiet.

"Shhh, listen," Tufte whispered. "There's so much texture between us and anything else. Now listen . . ."

He clapped his hands.

"Almost no reverb. It's an amazing and natural echo-free chamber."

Over the course of the visit, I became more fascinated by Tufte's almost childlike wonder and excitement than with anything he was pointing out.

We headed back out of the shady bamboo grove, into the bright sunlight, big puffy fair-weather clouds scudding across the treetops on the ridgeline. Tufte paused before parting, inhaled a big breath of the fragrant field before heading back inside. New York seemed to be far, far away.

Then, suddenly and unbidden, it was right there.

"Yeah, it's like a dream here," Tufte said, looking out to the hills. Then he turned, arms outstretched. "Biggest problem—there's no dim sum up here. None! I don't think there's any in Connecticut."

And with that, he was gone.

⫷◆⫸

Southwest out of Woodbury, Connecticut, Route 6 winds along through gentle green hills, past tidy hilltop farms facing out to panoramic views, as Litchfield County becomes northern Fairfield County.

It's ironic, really. Fairfield County is Connecticut's most populous, the one closest to the New York metro area, and contains four of the state's seven largest cities. Northern Fairfield County, however, contains only one of those cities (Danbury); the other, much larger three are all nearly 30 miles south along Interstate 95.

This upper little corner of the county is a place apart. The state's two largest lakes are here, creating a green landscape of water, woods, hills, all threaded with rambling roads through smaller towns like Redding Ridge, Weston, and Wilton. The quiet, mostly rural, slower pace of the area has long attracted those, especially artists, looking for a refuge from the city, yet one still within easy travel distance.

Painter Julian Alden Weir found all of that on a farm he bought in Wilton, Connecticut, just 10 miles from the New York border. Weir, a founding figure of the American Impressionism movement in the late nineteenth century, was inspired by the area's woods and meadows to create some of his most memorable works, like *Upland Pastures*, which hangs today in the Smithsonian Art Museum. On the farm, he enjoyed entertaining visitors like fellow painters Childe Hassam and John Singer Sargent. Weir died in 1919, but the grassy pathways, woods, and fields full of wildflowers look much like they did a century ago. Even his studio—brushes out, tubes of paint scattered on a table—looks like the artist merely got up to take a short break. Today, Weir Farm has the distinction of being America's only national park dedicated to American painting.

On a hot, hazy July morning, quiet and still but for the birds and the buzz of a cicada, I stand on a grass walking path where it crosses a sunny meadow of high, waving grass and goldenrod, before heading into a shady grove of stout, red maple trees. I am entranced by the sheer quiet, the simple natural beauty. It's easy to see why an artist would find this so appealing. Then, and now. On the back porch of the small, wooden house that serves as the visitor center, little kits of paints and brushes are left for visitors to use. Artists and would-be artists are encouraged to paint here still.

WEIR FARM NATIONAL HISTORICAL PARK, WILTON, CONNECTICUT.

"There's just something special about Weir Farm," says park ranger Kristin Lessard, as we stand in the bright summer sun next to the open barn door of the artist's original studio. "There's this beautiful, painterly light, and the landscape has been so well preserved."

"It truly seems unchanged," I marvel.

"Amazingly unchanged." She smiles. "So you're walking in the footsteps of these American masters, and it's like stepping back in time."

And yet, it might well have changed. Dramatically. From the spot on the path where I'm standing, drinking in the warm, green hush of meadow and woods, I might have heard the screech of a big truck's jake brake from just a mile off, as a barreling eighteen-wheeler exited a busy highway. Because that's exactly what might have been there.

"Yup. All these trees? Gone."

In neighboring Redding, Connecticut, only fifteen minutes from the meadows of Weir Farm, I'm standing along a sloping path through the woods with Mitch Ancona, a board member of the Norwalk River Valley Trail. Which, had events unfolded differently, wouldn't exist at all.

"It's stunning, really, when you think of it, right?" I say, letting my view turn in a slow arc around the woods. "A highway here."

"Yup—literally everything we're looking at here," Ancona says, shaking his head and spreading his arms wide. "Gone."

What's ironic is that the pretty path in the woods on which we stand is actually the final outgrowth of a proposed highway. In the 1960s, a plan was gaining momentum to turn State Route 7, a two-lane roadway which meanders the nearly 23 miles between Norwalk and Danbury, Connecticut, into "Super 7," a six-lane superhighway. By the 1970s, construction had begun in Norwalk. But fierce local opposition had also begun to build. Years of environmental impact statements, injunctions, and lawsuits slowly ground the project to a halt. Finally, in 2010, the state acceded to wide public pressure, and instead created funding for a 38-mile, multiuse recreational trail along much of the same path between the two cities. The Norwalk River Valley Trail was born.

"The great thing about this section right here, the Redding mile, is that you are really in the woods," says Ancona. "The Wilton section has a few more road crossings, but here, you're really in the woods, just riding right through the trees."

Ancona has brought a bike for me. We get both of them off his truck, helmets on, and we're off. Fast. Not sure how much dynamiting and leveling it would have taken to bring a road through here, but it takes no pedaling as we start out; we're going straight downhill, single file, through fairly dense woods.

"That's the other thing I like about this section," he says over his shoulder. "It's a bit undulating, more up and down, more winding and twisty, which is nice."

We stop briefly at the base of the hill, where the path straightens out and curves through the trees. A man walks briskly by us, his two walking poles clicking in time as he passes.

"Who uses the trail mostly, Mitch?"

"Everybody. From people like that, just walking and hiking, to cyclists, runners, and in winter, people cross-country skiing and snowshoeing. And families. My two daughters—they wouldn't want to go on some of the mountain bike trails I go on, but here—we can bike together, we can chat, we can have a shared experience, no worries about cars and traffic and things like that."

MITCH ANCONA, NORWALK RIVER VALLEY TRAIL, REDDING, CONNECTICUT. (BOB OLIVER)

Not here; not anymore.

As we ride, Mitch points up, where a hawk is circling; he's seen an eagle here as well. We come out to a road that separates the finished section we've been on from the still-to-be-completed section ahead of us. In the summer of 2022, about 30 percent of the trail was built out; the hope was that it would be 100 percent finished within ten years.

"This is my happy place," says Ancona, leaning on his bike and smiling, looking back at the trail. "On my bike, in the woods, a beautiful trail."

"A beautiful trail that was almost an ugly highway," I add.

"Pretty amazing, isn't it?"

It truly is. Success. Which is also how I feel about this unique corner of Connecticut. I had set out to find a part of the state near to New York that nonetheless evoked more of New England. And I found it. Along with some great people.

Now I just had to bike back uphill to my car.

THREE BROTHERS DINER & HOLIDAY DINER

(Danbury, CT)

THREE BROTHERS DINER, DANBURY, CONNECTICUT. (STANLEY KALLIVROUSIS)

On *one* street in Danbury, Connecticut, you'll find *two* storied diners. No city should be that lucky.

There's been a diner at 242 White Street since the 1930s. Forty years later, a young Greek immigrant named Nick Kallivrousis worked his way up to owning the diner, and it's been family-run ever since. Today, Nick's son Stanley (yes, there are three brothers) runs things.

There've been some changes. The exterior was returned to a classic chrome and neon look from the 1950s.

It's a clientele that values the authentic and the traditional.

"It's a diner-loving town," says Stanley. "Everybody's a diner person here."

And they know their way around. Stanley greets many entering customers by name; no menus are handed out. No need. Regulars? On an early, sunny spring morning, I pulled up a chair at a table of three older fellows who've been coming to the diner since its earliest days. Eight decades ago.

"Oh, yeah," says the trio's senior member, who's ninety-five. "We used to come here—can I say it?—way back when it was Durkin's."

Big laughs all around. But it gets pretty quiet when the food arrives. Big plates of pancakes, eggs, and French toast overloaded with whipped cream and strawberries will do that.

(*continued*)

At lunchtime, less than a mile down the street, another enticing sign beckons: "Holiday Diner." Who am I to resist such a siren call? Or relax into a comfy booth by the window and not feel delightfully at home?

"We have a very *Cheers*-like atmosphere. I probably know the name, or at least recognize, 90 percent of the people who walk through that door," says owner George Psarofagis, a cheerful, youthful, late-forty-something with short dark hair. "Like Bob over there, coming here for fifty years, way before we've been here. So many regulars. My job is to greet 'em and hand out menus, but most of 'em don't need them. I just stand around and tell jokes all day."

In truth, he does a lot more, but his day is no doubt a lot different now than when he worked in finance. His dad owned the diner, and as a kid, Psarofagis was put to work on weekends and after school. And every other opportunity.

"I was the only kid in America who hated snow days, because if it snowed and there was no school, we were going to work."

But after college, and starting his own career, Psarofagis missed the diner.

"It pulled me back. I love it. I love the people. I work way more hours now than I ever did before, but it doesn't bother me as much. It just seems more fulfilling."

The diner seems full of friends. Or maybe that's partly the way the owner laughs, ribs his regulars, and chats up one person after another.

There's been a diner on this end of White Street since 1947. Eventually the Danbury Diner, as it was called, became the Holiday Diner. Being closer to the New York metro area, the diner is more of that New York–New Jersey type; not a slim, cozy dining car, but a couple of dining areas, with the front made of a long counter and booths by the windows. The food is straight-up classic diner fare, but with some twists you don't see coming, like chicken and waffles, Oreo pancakes, or Philly steak quesadilla. In addition, Psarofagis has created his own unique play space on the menu: milkshakes.

"People have a certain expectation of a diner—comfort food—and they want that expectation to be met. I felt like milkshakes fall into that comfort-food zone. But we play around with it."

Let's just say chocolate, vanilla, or strawberry are for the uninitiated here.

Envelope-pushers might order a Cinnamon Toast Crunch or a cannoli milkshake. All the better to wash down that Philly steak quesadilla.

The lunch rush has died down, too.

George Psarofagis cashes out an older customer, gives him a hearty pat on his shoulder.

"Thank you, man. Take care of yourself, all right?"

This diner is uncommonly friendly, and it's aptly named. And this one street—with its two wonderful diners—is a diner lover's avenue of dreams.

CHAPTER 10

Finishing Strong (and Small):
On the Road in Little Rhody

Coming east from Connecticut on Interstate 95, destination southwest Rhode Island. Hardly the scenic route, but like Amtrak, easily the most direct: Long Island Sound on the right, whizzing by New Haven, Old Saybrook, New London, Mystic. At Westerly, over the Connecticut border and into Rhode Island.

Rhode Island is New England's (and the nation's) smallest state. It's also the second-most densely populated. Yet, surprisingly, there's a lot of open space in Rhode Island. Most of it just happens to be liquid.

The entire middle of the state is made up of Narragansett Bay and its marine estuary. An inlet of the Atlantic, the 147 square miles of the bay make up more than 15 percent of the state's total area, literally cleaving Rhode Island's land area in half. All that water has a way of making Rhode Island seem larger, more expansive, than it really is. Water—either the ocean itself, or the bay—seems always to be coming into view or peeking just over your shoulder as you drive. Nowhere in Rhode Island is the water prettier or more pronounced than in the state's South County and the 30 or so miles of continuous shoreline between Point Judith and Watch Hill.

NARRAGANSETT BAY, RHODE ISLAND.

S<small>OUTH</small> C<small>OUNTY SUNSET</small>, C<small>HARLESTOWN</small>, R<small>HODE</small> I<small>SLAND</small>.

These are the long sandy stretches and beaches–minus the dunes–most similar to those on Cape Cod and the Islands. In Westerly's village of Weeka-paug, I've often vacationed with my family, swimming and surfing with my kids at lovely little Fenway Beach. Just across the shore road, ringed with fragrant beach plum and connected to the ocean, many large salt ponds–Winnapaug, Ninigret, Quonochontaug ("Quonnie" to locals)–also dot the area.

Zipping north along busy Route 1, past Matunuck, passing storied Rhode Island fishing villages like Jerusalem, Galilee, and Point Judith. Six miles fur-ther, at Narragansett, the southern end of South County's most interesting waterway meets the ocean.

"It's like the state of Rhode Island–it's small and compact, but there's lots of really cool things in there."

Few people know the Narrow River better than Veronica Berounsky. A marine biologist, she moved here with her husband in the 1970s to work at the

University of Rhode Island's famed Graduate School of Oceanography. In a house on a small, grassy hill just above the riverbank in Narragansett, she raised her kids, and developed a deep and abiding love for a river the Native Narragansett Nation called "Pettaquamscutt."

Technically, as Berounsky is quick to point out, it's not a river. Covering just over 6 miles, from its lake-like headwaters in North Kingstown, to the sea in Narragansett, it's actually a tidal estuary, part salt water, part fresh. But it's undeniably narrow, appearing on the map like a curving thin blue gash, no wider than nearby Route 1, which it parallels. Although streams of summer tourists and visitors pass by it (and over it) on the way to South County beaches, it remains a remarkably quiet and uncrowded place. It's not unpeopled, though. Residents, like Berounsky, live all along its length.

VERONICA BEROUNSKY, NARROW RIVER, NARRAGANSETT, RHODE ISLAND. (NORA LEWIS / UNIVERSITY OF RHODE ISLAND)

And with all that, even for its relatively small footprint, it's an unusually diverse habitat. In the air above the river, gulls, cormorants, egrets, ospreys, and an occasional eagle soar. In the protected salt marsh of the John H. Chafee National Wildlife Refuge, smaller birds like willets and saltmarsh sparrows nest. In the water swim sea trout, salmon, and bass. And on the water, people paddleboard, fish, boat, canoe, and kayak. Veronica Berounsky has done all of that, and has even swum the entire length of the river on several occasions.

"I love being in and around the river. I love to swim in the river," she says with a laugh as we stand next to the water on the small wooden dock below her house. "I love knowing the water quality is good enough so that I'm fine swimming there as long as I want to."

I leave the swimming to Berounsky, but on a sunny mid-June morning, she and I do set out in a couple of kayaks. We paddle a bit north, away from the Middle Bridge. I follow her lead to a wider section. We are in the middle of the river. A river, it turns out, which is full of surprises.

"Deepest part of the river right, here," she says, pointing with her paddle for emphasis.

"How deep?"

"Twenty meters," she says.

"That is way deeper than I would have expected."

"I know." She nods. "If you took the Point Judith Lighthouse—which is fifty-one feet—and put it in here, it would disappear."

We paddle south, under the Middle Bridge. Here it narrows significantly; only about fifty feet across. Lush, tall green grasses overhang the water and tower around us. It's quiet, and the water looks clear and inviting.

For those, like Berounsky, who love being on it and in it, the quality of the river has long been a priority. She's an active leader of the decades-old Narrow River Preservation Association, which monitors the water, routinely testing it, and participating in the wider Watershed Watch program, run by the University of Rhode Island, which tracks the water quality of all the state's fresh- and salt water. With so many small hills along the river, Berounsky tells me, storm-water runoff remains an ongoing issue. Alas, the bigger threats to the river are not local, but global.

"We've seen a significant increase in water temperature over time," says Berounsky.

"So, the river's warming, like a lot of bodies of water, right?"

"Yes. The fact that we don't get ice out here in the winter like we used to, that's a sure sign. And then there's sea-level rise. Lot of people here with property right on the water; that's a real concern."

Still, on this day, on this unique river, it was pretty hard not to see what appeals so much to so many that live and play on it.

"There are so many different sections and moods to it," she says. "The light first thing in the morning, the sunsets, just sitting on my dock at night in the dark and quiet and suddenly seeing some bioluminescent fish in the water—you put your hand in the water, and they light up like a firefly. It's just a wonderful place."

-〈〈〈◆〉〉〉-

Just north of the Narrow River, Route 138 carries traffic over the Jamestown Verrazzano Bridge, and across Conanicut Island. It's a short crossing; no sooner off that bridge, and you're on the Newport Bridge, crossing over the heart of Narragansett Bay and onto its largest island, Aquidneck. Here, east-west 138 connects to north-south 114. At the southern end of the island is the

NARROW RIVER, RHODE ISLAND.

fabled city of Newport, famous for its equally fabled rich people's former summer homes. But that's a Gilded Age touristy thing. ("Cottages," the Astors and Vanderbilts called their seventy-room summer homes.) Newport's also a real place of rich history and enduring cultural traditions, like the historic and still-vital Redwood Library and Athenaeum (founded 1747), and the equally iconic annual Newport Folk and Jazz Festivals.

Newport is the southernmost of Aquidneck Island's three towns. Up through Middletown, it's 9 miles to Portsmouth, the island's northern end. While mostly flat, this is the island's highest ground; looking out, the ocean is the horizon.

There's something improbable about finding a farm on a 44-square-mile island in the middle of what's already the smallest state, where there's understandably little wasted space, and where every acre seems to be prized and zealously accounted for. Today, Rhode Island's remaining farms mostly raise other greenery: turf, shrubs, floral, and ornamentals.

Louis Escobar jokes that he didn't get the memo.

"Yeah, not very profitable, that's for sure," says Escobar, with a wince and a laugh as he tilts his trucker hat back and wipes his forehead in the warm mid-June sun. "Food production is Rhode Island's poorest agriculture."

"Lucky you," I say.

"Yeah, right—lucky me!"

For more than thirty years, Louis and his wife, Jane, have milked ninety-five cows on 98 acres that were farmed originally by Louis's dad. The challenges are many. Not only are they in food production in a state where that's vanishing, they're also dairy farmers, a once-hardy breed in New England whose numbers have shrunk dramatically for decades.

But Louis Escobar has an extra challenge that goes well beyond milk prices and the tough local landscape for food production. In 2015, he had a horrific accident on the farm. His tractor tipped over on him, leaving him a quadriplegic.

"C'mere," yells Louis over his shoulder. "Lemme show you something."

I follow, but he has a good head start. He tools around the farm today in a motorized wheelchair. It's an unusual sight. Farming—any farming, anywhere—is tough enough, period. Having livestock in particular demands long days that start before dawn, with little to no time off. Animals have to be fed and taken care of. Further, farming with livestock in a northern climate means doing those long days through long, cold winters that can make the already hard physical work even more punishing.

"We get up every day, we start milking right about quarter after five in the morning," says Jane. "And then it's run, run until you're done."

Yet, with all of that, and even after the accident, the couple never seriously thought about giving up.

"Never even a thought," Louis says, shaking his head. "I felt that we had good help here, and the farm is going to continue."

Gesturing at a row of cows near us, Jane is even more adamant. "To get rid of the farm at that point, to stop doing it, would have been just another nail in the coffin. He'd lost enough."

Curiously, Louis swears there's been an upside, too.

"Before my accident, at seventy-seven, I was less productive."

"So, wait," I interrupt. "You're saying you're actually *more* productive now than you were before the accident?"

"Yup. I have great help, but I also have more time to think about long-range things that need to be done, and then make those decisions."

Like helping to found Rhody Fresh, a local co-op that now produces its own brand of milk. The Escobars also operate a small inn on the property, they host private events, and each fall, a new corn maze sprouts in the fields. Call it "agritourism," call it survival—these are the things that small, local farms in New England have to do today to stay in business. You adapt. Or you go under.

"Some people say, how the heck do you do it?" says Jane Escobar. "You just keep going, that's all."

And they do. Louis has already had to get at least one new set of tires for his wheelchair. Jane tells me that he's chased down errant cows in the chair, and broken a rib once when it tipped over.

Louis Escobar, Portsmouth, Rhode Island (Carl Vieira)

Walking alongside Louis in his chair, I have to walk faster to keep up. He stops near the milking barn and looks out across a field. It's clear that he and Jane love what they do, and feel a deep and enduring connection to the farm, its history, and their place in it.

"I love the fact that we can keep it running," he says, more to himself than to me. "And it's doing as well as any dairy farm is going to do at this point."

And with that, and a grunt, he's off and rolling. Those cows aren't going to milk themselves.

-《《◆》》-

From Portsmouth, north to Providence, is a bit of a 30-mile detour, skirting the northeast edge of Narragansett Bay. There are many things I truly love about Providence, the state's capital city. Driving in and around it isn't one of them. (Only Worcester, with a similar highway through the city, has as many on and off ramps, and is just as maddening.)

Hasbro Children's Hospital sits on the city's south side, hard by both the highway and the Providence River. The hospital is home to a renowned medical staff. Yet one of its most beloved personnel has no formal medical training.

"I see kids, patients, a good chunk of the day," says Steve Brosnihan, standing in the hospital lobby. "I help take their mind off of other things, the stuff that scares and worries them."

Brosnihan is Hasbro Children's Hospital's resident cartoonist. He goes from room to room during his day, his young patients often breaking into the first smile of their day, knowing that this warm and gentle, soft-spoken man doesn't carry meds or medical devices, only a sketchbook and crayons. For a short period, the illness which has caused so much hurt and worry is made to disappear entirely, as they sketch together, laugh together, admire together the fantastical creation which appears on what was a blank white page only minutes earlier. Most of the patients Brosnihan visits with have cancer or leukemia of some sort. Some get better and go home. Some lose their battle.

In the spring of 2010, a young teen who had formed a bond with Brosnihan was about to be discharged. Brosnihan, who commutes to the hospital by bike, had an idea for a final good-bye. He told the boy to look for him from his hospital window at a certain time that evening, down below at a bus stop. There, at the appointed time, Brosnihan paused on his way and repeatedly flashed his bike lights up at the kid's window. Then, to his surprise, he saw the lights of the hospital room flash on and off. The boy was saying good-bye and good night right back.

"I said, Wow, that's him! That's his room!" says Brosnihan, recalling this Aha! moment with delight. "And I thought, wait a minute—if that worked once, it can work again, and I started doing it for other patients that I was visiting. Then I figured, Hey, maybe other people can get in on this, too."

And they have. In fact, the whole city has. Over more than a decade, it's been a steadily growing phenomenon known as "Good Night Lights." Its creator has been tireless—and clearly persuasive—in asking the city's residents, businesses, and public services to join in.

"One minute, blinking a light for one minute, once a night," says Brosnihan. "That's what I'm looking for. That's what I ask folks. And everyone has said, 'A minute? Yeah, we can do that.'"

Hotels, universities, private businesses, tugboats, bars and restaurants, every night at 8:30 p.m.—for one "magic minute," as it's called—shine, blink, and flash good night to the kids at Hasbro Children's Hospital. Many of the young patients look forward all day to not only seeing the lights but, with their own special flashlights in hand, to flashing their own "good night" right back.

"I would say it's great and amazing and they just make your day or night when you're watching them," says ten-year-old Abby Waldron. "Because it shows you that somebody is saying good night to you, and like, helping you through your whole experience in the hospital."

Waldron had been having a tough day. She was being treated at Hasbro for non-Hodgkin lymphoma. Her mom, sitting in one corner of her daughter's hospital room with Steve Brosnihan, has a tired and worried look. What parent wouldn't? But her face lightens noticeably as Abby becomes animated in telling me about Good Night Lights.

"So, you're not just like, 'Oh, I'm in a hospital, this is gonna be so boring, no friends,' you know?" she explains to me. "You can look forward to something every single night and not just be like, 'Oh, now we're gonna say good night.'"

"It's like the whole *city* is saying good night, right?" I ask.

"Yeah! You can look everywhere and literally all you see is flashing lights or something saying good night. It's so cool."

Abby's smiling now. So is her mom. So is Steve Brosnihan. Hell, so was I.

Turns out, many of those all around the city who found themselves participating in the nightly one-minute ritual were enjoying it as much as the kids at the hospital. Over by the river at the trendy Hot Club, customers are invited to take turns turning the club's outdoor neon sign on and off. At a nearby assisted-living residence on the city's waterfront, small but bright flashlights are handed out each night just before 8:30.

"It's an exciting time," a resident told me. "Knowing the kids are over there looking at us, and we're looking at them. We get so much joy out of it."

On Wednesday nights, the East Providence Police Department turns out as many cars as possible. On the edge of a park a few blocks from Hasbro Children's, they carefully line up their cars side by side, front ends facing the hospital.

"We try and get the whole shift over there, if we can," says Chief Chris Parella. He laughs. "It's funny; the ones you wouldn't think would be into this are the ones who are the softest about it. But hey, who doesn't have a place in their heart for kids who should be out playing, but who are sitting scared in a hospital room?"

Just before 8:30 on a chilly February night, I follow along with Steve Brosnihan, behind Abby Waldron and her mom, as they head up to the top floor of the hospital, to a big, open room lined with large windows. Forming a wide arc, the chairs are all pulled up next to the windows; a panoramic view of the city spreads out below, all twinkling white lights and a rushing river of tiny red taillights on the curving highway seven stories down.

Abby rushes into the room and goes directly to a chair.

"Is this your spot?" I ask.

"Yes, right here." She looks at her watch. Pauses. Then: "It's 8:30!"

The lights in the room go off. It's 8:30 on the dot. I look out. I wonder how, in a city full of lights, one could pick out specific flashing ones. I needn't have wondered. There they are.

"Mom, I think those are the seniors!" Abby points excitedly.

"Yup!" Her mom points through the window. "Hot Club."

Most of the kids have their own flashlights. Some pick out specific directions in which to wave their own good-night message. Steve Brosnihan leans in to me as he points.

"Watch over there—they're going to light 'em up, and I hear they have a surprise tonight, too."

Sure enough, a sudden burst of bright lights from the park. One by one, each patrol car's flashing roof lights begin spinning brilliantly, throwing the glow widely. Then, more light erupts—two big fire trucks have joined the show. The kids are waving their arms. Parents and medical staff exchange smiling glances and thumbs-up signs.

"What do you think of it tonight, Abby?" I ask.

"It's like a grand finale!"

And then, in a minute, it's over.

The room lights come on. The kids, mostly in bathrobes, some in wheelchairs, begin to shuffle back out in a slow, plodding exodus to the elevators. Back to sterile hospital rooms that are not the familiar bedrooms they miss so much, and not in houses with the people they miss so much. Excited kids waving flashlights become anxious young patients fighting a disease again.

"What do you think the kids get from this?" I ask Steve Brosnihan, as we begin walking down the stairs. "It's only a minute, after all."

"True," he says, "but I think they get a sense that there are people out there they don't know who care about the fact that they're in this building, being treated for something that has led them to be hospitalized. And I think they feel support from these anonymous signals in the dark. I do."

"I notice the older kids kind of just watch."

"Older kids get, well, more reflective about it," says Brosnihan. "They feel so many bad things are going on, they're so aware of that. But I also think they see this maybe, like, on any given night, something good can happen, that there are people who want me to remember that."

"At the same time," I say, "Lotta much older folks in there were grinning as much as the kids."

"If your child is sick, all you want is to see that child return to being a child. And a smile is the start of that. They're smiling at their child smiling."

With that, Steve pulls a bike helmet out of his pack. As he snaps it on and prepares to head off, we joke that things have come a long way from his solo bike-light flash to a single patient. A whole city now joins in. It's a truly unique and extraordinary thing, created by a kind and thoughtful man who had an ingeniously wonderful idea, and made it come to life.

As I head out myself into the chill night air, I look back up at the hospital's windows, mostly dark now. Tomorrow, patients like Abby Waldron may face another tough, painful, and discouraging day. But when the day is over, and before she goes to sleep, countless strangers across the nighttime city will remind her that they see her, that they want her to feel better. And for one magic minute, she will.

STEVE BROSNIHAN AND ABBY WALDRON, PROVIDENCE, RHODE ISLAND. (AMY WALDRON)

JIGGER'S DINER

(East Greenwich, RI)

JIGGER'S DINER, EAST GREENWICH, RHODE ISLAND.

Providence has long been a showplace of some nationally significant classic diners, like the Westside, and next door in Pawtucket, the venerable and iconic Modern Diner.

Fifteen miles south of Providence in East Greenwich, Rhode Island, Jigger's Diner is a gem that stands with the state's other great diners, even if it stands apart from big-city traffic. East Greenwich ("EG" to locals) is a lovely town, lots of great little stores, and a lot of water. Its Main Street runs along a hillside overlooking Greenwich Bay, a narrow finger inlet off of larger Narragansett Bay. Midway down Main, in all its light blue, classic chrome, and stainless-steel splendor, is Jigger's. It was opened by Vilgot "Jigger" Lindberg in 1917, and became instantly popular with locals. In 1950, the original diner was replaced with a larger, genuine Worcester dining car (#826). By the 1980s, the diner went through a succession of owners, and at one point was closed for more than a decade.

In 2012, Karie Myers reopened the diner and, as owner/chef, has overseen its return to stability and popularity as a fixture on Main Street, and the landmark it's always been, open or closed.

"I love my customers," says Myers at the counter, smiling as she waves to a familiar face that's just entered. "I get all the actual locals who come in all week, and not the swarms of tourists like Newport. It's much more approachable here. I've heard people call East Greenwich the 'anti-Newport.'"

It's tight inside, one row of booths along the narrow aisle that separates them from the counter. Breakfast is busy, the counter's full, and the fans are many.

"During the pandemic, she kept this open, and was unbelievable," says an older guy who drives down from Providence a few times a week. "Only takeout, but I'd get it and sit in my car out front, she'd wave. Now I'm inside again—and you don't leave hungry, lemme tell you!"

Myers does some new twists and tweaks on menu staples, offering her own take on traditional Rhode Island johnny cakes, and it's the only diner I've visited that offers latkes Benedict. As with all great diners, the comfort food is good, but it's the added comfort of community that makes Jigger's feel like a true gathering place, not just another place to eat.

"My grandmother worked here in the 1950s—her picture's right up there," a young woman in a booth points out to me. "When she passed away, I brought in a picture of her working here, and Karie put it in a frame and put it up. So now every time I come here, I think of my grandma."

From Providence, Interstate 195 curves south through Fall River, Massachusetts, where Route 24 South promptly darts back into Rhode Island. At Tiverton, Route 77 winds south 10 miles or so to Little Compton, itself a lovely little town on the water, bordered by the Sakonnet River and the ocean. (With a wonderful little general store, Wilbur's, too.)

As it happens, I was in Little Compton to visit yet another Rhode Island hospital. And on a chilly and wet early-spring morning, there was the sign at the edge of a dirt driveway: "Antique Stove Hospital." The patients were all arrayed on the muddy grass before me.

Imagine a sprawling junkyard filled not with old cars, but old stoves. Really old stoves. Dead stoves. I wonder what makes this a stove *hospital* versus a stove cemetery. Where, I wonder, are the "doctors" saving these things?

"Good morning! C'mon inside, get outta the rain!"

I follow Emery Pineo into a low, garage-like building. Pineo is a quick-moving, spry guy of eighty or so. He's got white hair beneath a black, wool Greek fisherman's cap, and he's wearing a beat-up old work jacket.

"Little warmer and dryer in here, huh?" He smiles.

A lot warmer and dryer.

The door opens suddenly, and a big, younger guy stands there.

"You made it!"

Brandon Pineo is Emery's son. Husky, over six feet, in a flannel jacket with a well-worn brown tweed scally cap on his bald head.

"I guess you could call this our showroom!" says Emery, laughing.

You could. The entire room is filled with old stoves. Unlike most of the rusting relics outside, these stoves have all been repaired and refurbished. Most will run with wood, some with coal. They'll all be sold, if they haven't been already, and they'll all be used anew by someone who, presumably, lives in a house with other, more modern appliances and conveniences. They're all old—a century or more—but they're all shiny and gleaming with brass and chrome, and they all look strangely brand-new.

I admire the ornate heat gauge on a "Modern Glenwood E," which no doubt was the hip look of modernity itself when it came off the line in 1905.

"That's a beauty, that one," says Brandon, running his hand over the smooth range top. "They made those into the 1930s with no changes. None."

Brandon's a former high school physics teacher. He'd always helped out his dad, and then, some years back, decided to help him full-time. His dad has loved stoves and all that they represent since he was a kid.

"My job when I was a kid was to take my bicycle on Saturday morning, go across the river to the widow Lawrence's, and get eggs," recalls Emery. "And she had an old, wood-burning kitchen range and she was always baking cookies or biscuits or something because she knew all the kids were coming Saturday morning. I always wanted that stove."

He didn't get it.

"She passed away when I was about twelve, and before she was in the ground, that stove was in the dump. So, I missed that one," he says, shaking his head slowly and ruefully, as if the disappointment is fresh, not fifty or more years old. "So eventually, when I got old enough, I said, You know, I want one of those ranges, and I went out and I bought one that was a piece of junk and I paid way too much for it. But in the process of fixing it, I met all the right people. And the next thing you know, people are bringing me stoves—'Could you fix this one?'—and now I got a house full of stoves!"

And a yard full. And a couple of garages full. Brandon lives nearby; the two work all day on refurbishing the old stoves.

EMERY AND BRANDON PINEO, LITTLE COMPTON, RHODE ISLAND.

"We're well over a year behind right now," says Brandon. "But once we actually lay our hands on the stove, depending on the range, and depending if there's some plating—'cause that we send out—it usually takes about nine days from start to finish for the whole job to be completed."

Some days they go on field trips to see a stove someone's getting rid of. They're selective now about what they fix. Ironically, in their work they use some state-of-the-art machines, as well as some cutting-edge green technologies. Their customers these days run the gamut, from those who want to go greener themselves, reducing their carbon footprint, to those who want to leave no prints at all.

"Yeah, we get some folks who've bought ten or fifteen acres somewhere," says Brandon, "and they're raising their own food, they're educating their own kids, and they want to go completely off the grid."

And the Pineos have a stove for them. But some of the same things that attract those folks are increasingly attracting others, even those very much *on* the grid.

"I'd say most of our customers, whoever they are, are people who are just very disappointed with a lot of modern products," says Emery. "They've had modern, even expensive stoves, and eventually, if they investigate, they land on the fact that many of these antique stoves were designed far better and more efficiently than anything that's available today."

It's not that stove designers lost their skill. Manufacturers, rather, craved the sales revenue lost to stoves that were simply made too well to break down. By the late 1940s, corners were cut, inferior parts were substituted for sturdy, unbreakable ones. The frustrating phenomenon known to modern consumers as "built-in obsolescence" was born.

"Modern stoves—products today—let's face it," grins Brandon, "they have that meeting about, okay, how we gonna make this fail in five to seven years? These stoves were designed to hold up. They were designed to be readily repaired, piece by piece, and able to be used over many generations."

But I'm less interested in the stove mechanics as I am with some of the history here. Most of the stoves are a century old, but some are significantly older, and of museum quality. Brandon has become something of a curator of these pieces, and I eagerly follow him up a narrow wooden staircase in the storage garage to the upper floor. Scattered about are the rusting carcasses of dozens of old stoves and parts, but Brandon makes a beeline for the far corner of the attic-like space near the window.

"Currently, this is the oldest one in our collection. It's late 1600s."

It stands less than four feet tall, with four legs supporting a small "stove" compartment. In size and shape, it resembles a thin side table. A small, hinged-metal door, still functioning, is where one would have added either wood or coal. According to Brandon, it's made of sheet iron that's been sourced to Eastern Europe's Ural Mountains.

"This would have been imported from the Old World," he says, brushing some dust aside. "If you look at some early documents of the first settlers here, many would say, 'If you come to the New World, procure a German or a Dutch stove.' That's what this one is."

It has handles, and was meant to be mobile.

"At the time period, the cost of making sheet metal was so expensive, the stoves were made in such a fashion that one would be able to pick them up and move them from chamber to chamber, rather than having multiple stoves."

Essentially, a four-hundred-year-old space heater.

"Something, huh? Just an amazing piece of history."

In essence, the Antique Stove Hospital is as much a museum as a business. But it's something more, as well. It's also a celebration of something that was once a calling card in New England: genuine craftsmanship. Emery and Brandon Pineo have a passion for both the craft of an earlier age, and for their own craftsmanship in preserving these pieces and giving them new life for a new age.

"You know," says Emery, tilting his cap back on his head, "you start with something that's basically bound for the scrapyard and turn it into something that's useful again."

"Every single one of these stoves was responsible for some family's survival over the years," says Brandon, nodding in agreement with his dad. "So to be able to restore one of these stoves and bring it back . . ."

His thought trails off. He smiles, patting the restored century-old stove he's been sitting on. "This'll still be working long after I'm gone. I guess that's my contribution to the world."

⸺⟨⟨⟨◆⟩⟩⟩⸺

Back on the road, in a gray, chilly mist. Fitting.

Nearby, in the little village of Adamsville, I pause for a moment in passing a special place: Gray's General Store.

Opened in 1788, it was the nation's longest continuously operating general store when it closed in 2012. Alas, not every store—or stove—can be saved. Most things, like people, have their time. But pulling away from the dark and shuttered store and having just left the warmth where some old things *are* being saved, I had to smile at the irony. Here in the region's smallest state, I was reminded of some big, and enduring, truths about New England.

The past matters deeply here. It helps to define New England. But it doesn't designate it as some sort of six-state historical landmark. Progress, new ideas, new people, innovation, and reinvention also define New England. Always have. Consider the American Revolution, Abolitionism, the telephone, first public park, and for that matter, Brandon and Emery Pineo and their yard full of old stoves awaiting new life. What no longer works—from outdated ideas to outdated machines—is dispensed with. What's worth holding on to—hard work, honoring the past while embracing the future, caring about quality and crafts-manship, and above all, a strong sense of community—thankfully, endures here.

Above all, New England is an authentic place. Both at its best, and in its faults and flaws. The people I've met on my travels, and who've impressed me most, are all of that. Each of them defines New England, too. Throw in a few good diners, and it's no wonder that I, too, have loved so much to call this place home.

ACKNOWLEDGMENTS

This is my fifth book published by Rowman & Littlefield. Of those, it's the fourth published under their Globe Pequot imprint. I appreciate that relationship which has been forged over a decade. On this project, thank you to editorial director David LeGere, assistant acquisitions editor Kate Ayers, production editor Alden Perkins, and copyeditor Melissa Hayes.

It's important to note that most of the stories in this book are ones that I reported on and produced for television. Meaning that, before all of the print in the preceding pages, there was a lot of video created to tell these stories. And that was the work of the talented photographers with whom it's been my privilege to work at *Chronicle*, Boston's longtime nightly newsmagazine. Thank you to Carl Vieira, Judi Guild, Bob Oliver, Rich Ward, and Jennifer Platt-Ure. Thanks as well to editors Ellen Boyce, Deb Therrien, Brian Menz, and Rick LeBlanc; to graphic designer Tony Lathrop; and to executive producer Julie Mehegan. And thank you to both Art Donahue and Mark Kanegis, both longtime friends and colleagues, both also two of New England's most magnificent photographers.

Each of these stories involve people who gave their time, effort, and cooperation in my own efforts as a journalist and storyteller. I am forever grateful. These people have made a deep and lasting impression on me. The proof is this book. Thank you.

Saving my deepest gratitude for last, thank you to my family: my wife, Anne-Marie, and my daughters, Kyra and Daisy. Your patience, support, and love mean everything. And I promise to cull my ever-growing collection of diner mugs. (Eventually.)

-‹‹‹•›››-

INDEX

ABOUT THE AUTHOR

Ted Reinstein has been an award-winning reporter for *Chronicle*, Boston's celebrated—and America's longest-running, locally produced—nightly newsmagazine since 1997. He also sits on WCVB's editorial board, and has been a contributor to the station's political roundtable show, *On The Record.* His previous books include *New England Notebook*, *Wicked Pissed*, and (with Anne-Marie Dorning) *New England's General Stores* (all published by Globe Pequot). He's also the author of *Before Brooklyn: The Unsung Heroes Who Helped Break Baseball's Color Barrier* (Lyons Press).

-⋘◆⋙-